THE TUDORS

Jon Nichol

Basil Blackwell · Oxford

CONTENTS

INTRODUCTION

THE TUDORS is an outline course on British history from about 1480 to 1600. In rough date order pages 2-39 handle major political, military and religious themes: for example, the character of the different kings and queens – Henry VII, Henry VIII, Edward VI, Queen Mary and Queen Elizabeth; battles such as Bosworth and the threat from the Armada; and the break away from the Roman Catholic church and the setting up of the Church of England.

Pages 40-63 look at two major Tudor topics: the Tudor village and the Tudor town, including London. *The Tudor Village* is based upon a number of typical examples, and aims to reconstruct the changes which went on in the countryside during the Tudor era. *The Tudor Town* is largely about the county town of Shrewsbury in Shropshire, but also draws upon evidence about similar towns in other parts of the country. It deals with London separately.

THE TUDORS emphasises the handling of historical **EVIDENCE**. Each subject encourages you to think about the clues the past has left behind and, on the basis of them, to work out your own ideas about the Tudor era.

The book is carefully arranged for class, group or individual work. Each page or double page is self-contained, and provides material for topic work. The questions are roughly graded for difficulty, and give scope for pupils who work at different speeds. Questions are carefully designed to encourage you to build up your own mental picture of the past.

History is made up from *evidence* from the past, which we use to come to our own conclusions. Look at one historical clue, **A**, about an incident in Tudor history. Below are some points about this clue. Read each point in turn, and then try to answer the question at the end of it.

a The clue is a photograph of some remains which had been buried. What are they?
b They are from the bodies of two children whose skulls and bones were found. Doctors tell us that the children were from nine to fourteen years old when they died. How might they have died?
c The skulls and bones were found buried at the bottom of a staircase in the Tower of London, a royal prison. Who could the children have been?
d At the top of the staircase is a room in which two royal princes, Edward and Richard, lived in 1484. At about this time they disappeared, never to be seen again. Whose skulls and bones might have been buried at the bottom of the staircase?
e Prince Edward was the heir to the throne. Several nobles wanted to be king instead of him. If the skulls and bones at the bottom of the staircase are those of him and his younger brother, Richard, how might they have died?

Pages 2-3 tell you more about the mystery of the bones found in the Tower of London.

A

1

MURDER!
THE PRINCES IN THE TOWER

Background From 1450, for over fifty years, England's two most powerful noble families, those of YORK and LANCASTER, fought over which should rule England. This struggle is called the Wars of the Roses. (See *The Middle Ages*, also by Jon Nichol.) After a twenty-two year reign, the Yorkist king died in 1483. He had two sons, aged ten and twelve. The older, Edward, was too young to rule, so his uncle Richard ran the country for him, as regent. Richard was crowned King Richard III. In 1485 the Lancastrian leader, Henry Tudor, killed Richard III at the Battle of Bosworth (see pages 6-7). By 1486 the princes had disappeared. For three years they had lived in the Tower of London. What had happened to them? Most historians think that their uncle, Richard III, had murdered them. But how do we know? What clues are there? Let us pretend that we are trying Richard III in an imaginary court – the Court of History.

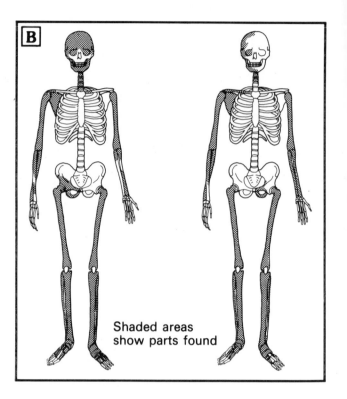

Shaded areas show parts found

Prosecutor: Richard III, you are on trial. The charge is murder – that in 1484 you ordered the deaths of the sons of Edward IV. They were prisoners in the Tower of London. How do you plead – guilty or not guilty?

Richard III: Not guilty.

Prosecutor: You will have chances to ask questions later. We now call our first witness, Domenico Mancini, an Italian visitor to London in 1484. Mr. Mancini, what did you write in your diary about Edward and Richard, the Princes in the Tower?

Mancini: They were taken into the inner part of the Tower. . . . Day by day they were seen less often behind the bars and windows, until at last they were seen no more.

Prosecutor: Call our second witness, a Londoner. In 1484 what did you write in your diary about the Princes?

A Londoner: After Easter there was much whispering among the people that the king had put the children of King Edward to death. . . . There were many different ideas about how they died. Some said that they were suffocated between two feather beds, others that they were drowned in malmsey (a wine), and others that a powerful poison killed them.

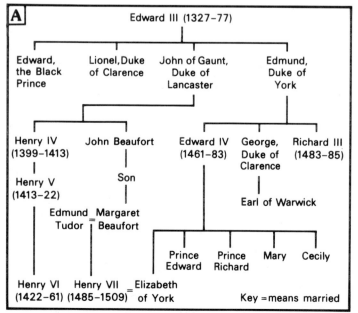

A

Edward III (1327–77)

| Edward, the Black Prince | Lionel, Duke of Clarence | John of Gaunt, Duke of Lancaster | Edmund, Duke of York |

Henry IV (1399–1413) — John Beaufort   Edward IV (1461–83) — George, Duke of Clarence — Richard III (1483–85)

Henry V (1413–22)   Son   Earl of Warwick

Edmund Tudor = Margaret Beaufort

Prince Edward   Prince Richard   Mary   Cecily

Henry VI (1422–61)   Henry VII (1485–1509) = Elizabeth of York

Key: = means married

C

D

Prosecutor: Our next witness is Sir Thomas More. In 1513, Sir Thomas, you lived at the court of King Henry VIII, Henry Tudor's son. You claimed that in 1484 one of King Richard's knights, Sir James Tyrell, ordered two of his men to go into the Princes' bedroom. What, Sir Thomas, did you say happened next?

Sir Thomas More: They wrapped them up in their bedclothes. They pushed the feather bed and pillows hard into their mouths. . . . After the wretches saw that they were dead, they stretched them naked on the bed and fetched Sir James to see them. . . . He got the murderers to bury them at the bottom of the stairs.

Richard: This is a pack of lies.

Prosecutor: Quiet! Now we will look at four exhibits.

A King Richard III's family tree. It shows what he would gain from the Princes' deaths in 1484.
B The bones of two boys, aged about eleven and thirteen, the Princes' ages in 1484. Workmen found these bones in 1674 when they knocked down the staircase which led to the Princes' bedroom.
C A drawing of the Tower of London in 1550, as Domenico Mancini would have seen it.
D An aerial photograph of the Tower of London, showing where the Princes lived.

? ? ? ? ? ? ? ? ? ? ? ?

1 Tell the story of what might have happened in the Tower, as if you were the prosecutor. Use these words to help you: plan; staircase; oak door; creaking; asleep; feather bed; floorboards; blankets; struggle; bodies; flagstones; shovel; Sir James Tyrell.

2 If you were helping King Richard to defend himself against the charge of murder, what questions might you ask about the *evidence* against him? Make out a table like **E**, with your points in the *Questions and Queries* column.

E

Evidence	Questions and Queries
Domenico Mancini	
A Londoner	
Sir Thomas More	
Exhibit **A**	
B	
C	
D	

3 What do you think happened to the Princes in the Tower? Use any books, pamphlets and collections of documents you can find to help you.

THE BATTLE OF BOSWORTH

Think of the last time you saw two teams playing football, rugby or hockey. Who won? Why? Try to recall the details. How well can you remember? On 22 August 1485 there was a contest between two different kinds of teams at Bosworth Field, Leicestershire. The two armies fought for a huge prize – the throne of England. Why were they fighting? Who was there? What happened?

Background King Richard III had many enemies. The main one was Henry Tudor, head of the LANCASTRIANS. Henry lived abroad, waiting for a chance to strike. This came in the summer of 1485. Many nobles would help him fight Richard III. He had killed or jailed members of their families. On 7 August 1485 Henry Tudor landed at Milford Haven, Wales. He marched to Bosworth through: Pembroke, Haverford, Cardigan, Aberystwyth, Machynlleth, Welshpool, Shrewsbury, Stafford and Tamworth. All the time men joined his growing army. At Bosworth, Henry Tudor came face to face with the army of Richard III.

The Armies As well as Henry Tudor's and Richard III's armies, there was a third force at Bosworth – that of the Stanleys. They were a noble family. No one knew whom they would back. To make sure of their help Richard III kept members of their family with him as hostages. How do you think the Stanleys felt about this? All three armies were made up of knights, foot-soldiers and archers. You can read more about the way in which they fought in *The Middle Ages*. You can see what it was like in picture **A**, drawn at about the time of the Battle of Bosworth.

Evidence about the Battle We know where the battle was fought – at Ambien Hill, map **B**. Polydore Vergil wrote the *only* description of the battle at the time it happened. He relied upon what men who were there told him, for he was not present. From his account and from the battlefield map, we will try to work out what happened.

The Battle Polydore Vergil wrote that Richard III drew up his troops on Ambien Hill.

Behind him were the men of the Earl of Northumberland, one of his nobles.

C *King Richard put his archers (like a strong fence and ditch) in front of his footmen and cavalry. Behind this leading force the King followed with a hand-picked group of men.*

Henry Tudor also got ready to fight:

D *. . . in front he had a small advanced force of archers. . . . He needed the backing of the Stanleys' army – about 3000 men, for he had barely 5000 soldiers. The King had twice as many and more.*

At about 10.30 a.m. Richard's and Henry's armies closed in.

E *The King ordered his soldiers to charge. They let out a great cry, and fired their arrows. Now followed hand-to-hand fighting with swords.*

By midday the battle was undecided. The Earl of Northumberland's men stayed on the top of Ambien Hill, watching the fight. The Stanleys' army began to close in fast on the fighting forces of Henry Tudor and Richard III. Whom would they back? Polydore Vergil wrote:

F *Richard drew near to Henry, and burning with anger, he spurred on his horse. Henry saw King Richard approaching. . . . King Richard killed several in his first charge, and threw down Henry's standard and its bearer, William Brandon. Then he fought John Cheney, a much stronger man than most. He stood against the King, who*

with great strength smashed him to the ground. Henry held out against the charge much longer than his men thought possible. They began to give up hope. . . .

But look! William Stanley came to the rescue with 3000 men. In a flash King Richard's men fled. He was left alone, fighting manfully in the thickest press of his enemies.

Richard III was killed. His crown was found in a bush, and placed on the head of Henry Tudor. Henry was the new king of England – Henry VII. Members of his family – the Tudors – were to rule England for the next hundred and eighteen years.

1 Copy a map from an atlas to mark the route of Henry Tudor from Milford Haven to Bosworth field. What kinds of problems do you think Henry would have had on his two-week march?

2 Either draw a plan of the battlefield **B** or cut out the different forces in the size shown on the key. On your own plan of **B** place where you think the different forces were at the start of the battle. Use the *evidence* on these pages to say how you think the battle went.

3 What would you have advised Richard III to have done at midday? He knows that the Earl of Northumberland has not moved. Should Richard:
   a retreat towards Northumberland;
   b approach the Stanleys for help;
   c retreat a little, gather his men together and try and break through to Henry Tudor. Put **a – c** in order of choice, and give reasons for your advice.

4 Write down what thoughts might have been going through Henry Tudor's mind as Richard III killed John Cheney. Look at **A**, and use these words to help you: army; number of troops; weapons; Richard's army; the Stanleys; treachery; retreat; attack; archers; footsoldiers; knights; outnumbered; wounds; screaming; blood; Brandon.

5 Why did Richard lose the battle?

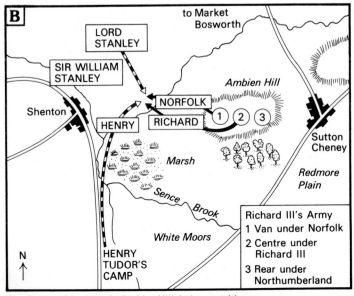

The Battle of Bosworth, Ambien Hill, Leicestershire

REBELLION! THE THREAT TO THE THRONE

After Bosworth King Henry VII – Henry Tudor – was still in danger. The Tudors only had weak links with the old English ruling dynasty. Evidence on pages 2-3 helps you see why. Edward IV's heirs claimed that they had a much better right to the throne than Henry Tudor. If women could inherit the crown, which of Edward IV's daughters do you think had first claim? If men could, which of his nephews?

Henry's main threat was from this previous reigning family of **York**. Map **A** shows other dangers to him. List **B** refers to the numbers on Map **A**.

The Yorkists' best plan was either to support the Earl of Warwick or to back a young man who pretended to be one of Edward IV's sons, Edward and Richard, the Princes in the Tower. By 1486 they had disappeared. No one could be certain that they were dead. In 1487 Yorkist nobles backed the claim of Lambert Simnel that he was the Yorkist heir to the throne. Lambert sailed with a force of German soldiers to Ireland to get the help of Irish nobles. With an Irish and German army he then invaded England. Henry VII defeated and captured Lambert in June 1487 at the bloody battle of Stoke. Twenty-five years later a Tudor historian tells us:

> C *Lambert is still alive to this very day. He has been promoted to trainer of the king's hawks. Before that he was for a time a turn-spit and did other foul jobs in the kitchen.*

Henry VII faced many threats to the throne. In 1491 the most serious pretender emerged, Perkin Warbeck. He claimed to be Prince Richard, the younger Prince in the Tower. In 1495 Margaret of Burgundy helped him to invade England. Henry VII routed his troops, and Perkin fled to Ireland and then to Scotland.

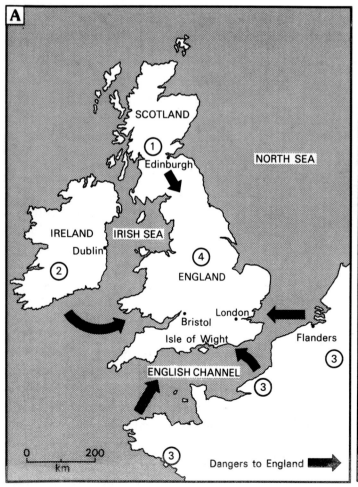

A

B

1 Scotland The Scottish kings were always ready to fight any English attempt to conquer them. Support of Henry's enemies would help their cause.

2 Ireland English efforts to subdue Ireland had failed. Irish barons would be willing to back Henry's enemies.

3 Burgundy/France Queen Margaret of Burgundy was a member of the family of York. Her country was a base for Henry's enemies. The kings of France could also back them if England and France quarrelled.

4 English Nobles Families who had fought Henry at Bosworth had much to lose. They might prefer to help Henry's enemies overthrow him.

In 1497 the Scottish King helped Perkin to invade England again, but he was caught, and later thrown into the Tower of London. A fellow prisoner was the Earl of Warwick. Warbeck and Warwick plotted to escape and overthrow Henry VII. They were captured, tried and executed. The main danger to Henry VII was over — but for the rest of his reign other members of the York family still claimed the throne.

???????????????????????????????

1 Draw three cartoons to show the adventures of Perkin Warbeck:
  a his 1497 attack on England;
  b his imprisonment in the Tower;
  c his execution.

2 Imagine you were advising Henry VII after his victory at Bosworth. List, in order of importance, plans **a – f** for stopping a rebellion. Give reasons for the order you choose and the points in favour of each plan.
  a Have a magnificent coronation, and make all English noblemen promise to obey the King.
  b Make peace with neighbouring countries — particularly France and Scotland.
  c Conclude treaties with foreign powers to increase trade in wool cloth and income from customs duties.
  d Marry the most important Yorkist alive, Elizabeth, the oldest sister of the Princes in the Tower.
  e Rule as efficiently and carefully as possible to pay for an army in case of war.
  f Make sure that the nobles do not keep private forces of archers, foot-soldiers and knights, and that they knock down their private castles.

3 Let's see how successful you would have been as a plotter against Henry VII. You need a coin and some paper for a diary of your attempt to seize the throne.

You are a pretender to the throne. Look at the possible areas of support for you on map **A** and Table **B**.

Choose any *two* of them. Enter them in your diary, and say how well you hope to do. To see how your rebellion is going, toss a coin for each of your chosen plans in list **1 – 4**. Table **D** shows how your plot has got on. Write a diary entry for month three of your rebellion.

D

Month Three

1 *Heads:* The Scottish king has decided to let you recruit a thousand soldiers in Scotland to sail with you to Cornwall to join a rebellion against King Henry.
Tails: The Scottish king has decided to stop helping you, as an English army is poised to invade Scotland. Also he hopes to marry Henry VII's youngest daughter, Princess Margaret.

2 *Heads:* The Irish lords have agreed to back a rebellion against Henry VII. They want Irish independence and will send soldiers to fight in England to help gain this.
Tails: Your main Irish supporter, Sir James Ormond, has just been killed in a brawl. Other Irish lords now refuse to back you.

3 *Heads:* Margaret of Burgundy has welcomed your plot, and has agreed to provide you with men, ships, money and arms with which to invade England. Rulers of other European countries accept you as England's rightful king.
Tails: Margaret of Burgundy cannot supply any men, ships and arms for your plans. Other rulers of Europe do not want to upset King Henry VII of England.

4 *Heads:* Noblemen at Henry VII's court — in particular the Yorkist Earl of Lincoln, and Sir William Stanley — are willing to join a plot against Henry. Sir William is a strong ally: his soldiers won the battle at Bosworth for Henry.
Tails: Henry has discovered the plot against him. Lincoln and Stanley are in the Tower, as is the Earl of Warwick, the main Yorkist claiment to the throne. Your chances of a successful rising in England are slight.

HENRY VII

What kind of person is our queen, Elizabeth II (1953-)? How can we find out about her? We use clues or evidence to tell us. We can also use evidence to discover how Henry VII ruled and what he was like. Pages 2-7 give us many clues. There are more below.

1 What people said In 1489 the Spanish Ambassador wrote a letter home:

> **A** *He (Henry VII) likes to be spoken about and looked up to by the whole world. In this he fails because he is not a great man. Although he claims many virtues, his love of money is too great. He spends all the time he is not in public or in his Council in writing his accounts of his expenses with his own hand.*

In May 1509 at Henry's funeral the preacher said:

> **B** *In politics no one was as wise as him. He had a very good memory, a quick and alert mind, and always gave fair and short reasons. . . . Many were the languages he spoke.*

He was friendly. He had a clear skin and blue eyes. With all Christian princes he made alliances. His might was feared everywhere, both inside and outside his kingdom.

By the people he was obeyed as much as any other king. For many a day his land lived in peace and quiet. In battle his success against his enemies was almost miraculous. During danger he calculated in a cold and clever way. He got wind of any treason plotted against him. Immense were his treasures and riches, and fair his buildings in the latest style.

2 What he wished people to think he looked like Government portraits reflect Henry VII's wishes. In 1486 he married Elizabeth of York. After Elizabeth died in 1503 Henry hoped to marry again, as he only had one son. The painting **C** is a picture he sent to a possible new wife.

3 His control over government money **D** is a page from an account book of one of his councillors — his main ministers. On the right-hand side of the page are the king's initials.

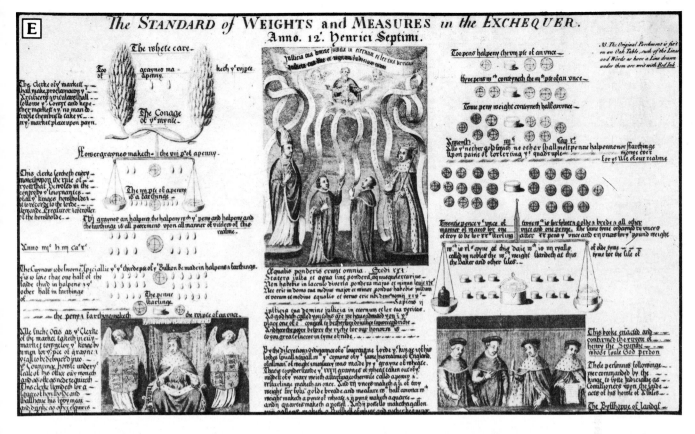

The STANDARD of WEIGHTS and MEASURES in the EXCHEQUER.
Anno. 12º. Henrici Septimi.

4 His interest in trade

As well as making trading treaties, in 1487 he passed a law stopping the export of cloth in an unfinished state. 1487 also saw the statute laying down standard weights and measures for traders. **E** gives an idea of what it involved.

5 How he ruled

Henry gained the backing of all of England's noble families. A modern historian tells us that in 1509 they were:

> **F** *A solid body of men, settled upon their lands, active in their counties which they ruled sometimes in conflict with one another but more commonly by agreement. . . .*

At court Henry ruled through the *council* and his *courts*. His council was made up from twenty to thirty ministers. Henry chose them from bishops, landed gentlemen and his nobles, if they worked hard and ran his affairs in a business-like way. To keep control of the North of England, the Welsh borders (or Marches) and Devon and Cornwall, Henry set up three local councils: those of the North, the Marches and the South West.

In the counties Henry VII relied upon his nobles and local gentry. The gentry made up some six to seven hundred JPs – Justices of the Peace. The JPs enforced the law in local courts and kept the peace.

6 His use of Parliament

From 1485-1497 Parliament met ten times: each session lasted about six weeks. Parliament represented all the country's leading landowners and townspeople. Henry used it in 1485 to confirm his right to the throne, and later to pass laws about the cloth trade, taxes, weights and measures, enclosures (see pages 48-49) and money. After 1497 Parliament only met once.

? ? ? ? ? ? ? ? ? ? ?

1 *Either*: towards the end of Henry VII's life Polydore Vergil described him as having, "*small, blue eyes; only a few poor blackish teeth; thin, white hair and a pale face*". Draw and colour in accurately Henry's face. *Or*: Look carefully at Henry's portraits, and describe in detail what you think they are trying to tell you about him.

2 Use the *evidence* on this page, and on pages 6-7 to write your own account of what you think Henry VII was like. Mention the clues and points 1-6, his skill as a soldier and how he dealt with rebellions and plotters.

HENRY VIII

What was Henry VIII, the new, young, king like in 1509? Born in 1492 he had been heir to the throne since the death in 1501 of Arthur, his older brother. The historian G. R. Elton tells us that by 1509 Henry VIII was:

A . . . *England's most tireless horseman, foremost wrestler, a first-class archer and hawker and jouster.*

Life at court was a whirl of feasting, jousting, hunting and dancing. In 1515 a diplomat from Venice met the young King, and wrote:

B *He wore a cap of crimson and velvet in the French way. The brim was tied up with lace loops, which had gold enamel tags. His doublet was in the Swiss fashion, with stripes of white and crimson satin. Scarlet were his tights. . . . Close around his neck was a gold collar from which hung a round cut diamond, the size of the largest walnut I ever saw. From this hung a most beautiful and very large round pearl. His cloak was of pure velvet lined with white satin, the sleeves open with a train more than four*

metres long. Around his cloak was thick gold cord, from which hung thick gold tassels.

C is a portrait of Henry at about this time, **D** his armour, and **E** shows him jousting. Another eye-witness tells us:

F *He is very talented, a good musician, composes well, . . . speaks good French, Latin and Spanish, is very religious, hears three masses daily when he hunts and sometimes five on other days. . . . He is very fond of hunting, and never takes his sport without tiring eight or ten horses. . . .*

What kind of ruler was Henry VIII during the first twenty years of his reign? Henry was interested in war. In 1510 he married the Spanish princess, Catherine of Aragon, who had been the wife of his dead brother. With Spain as an ally, England's old enemy, France, was a natural target. War broke out in 1512 and in 1513 Henry sailed to France with an army. An Englishman wrote twenty years later:

G . . . *he marched forward in good battle order through the Low Country until he came to the strong town of Therouanne. This he besieged and assaulted it so fiercely with continuous attacks that within a short time he forced them to yield the town.*

Henry marched on, and took the fort of Tournai. In a brief skirmish with a French army he captured a number of prisoners. Because the French ran away so quickly it is called the Battle of the Spurs.

England was also at war with the Scots. In 1513 the Scottish king was killed and his army destroyed at the Battle of Flodden. Peace came

in 1514. Then in 1518 Henry sold Tournai back to the French at a loss, and in 1522 again went to war with France and Scotland. Although 1525 saw peace, it was with no gains and with huge bills. Peasants rebelled against paying heavy taxes to meet the war's costs. A peasant from Kent said that Henry VIII had:

H . . . *not one foot of land more in France than his most noble father had, who lacked no riches nor wisdom to win the kingdom of France if he had thought it sensible.*

At home Henry showed no mercy to enemies or possible rivals to the throne. **I** shows what happened to some of them.

I

Date Name	Offence	Fate
1510 Richard Empson and Henry Dudley	Ministers who raised money for Henry VII – accused of treason	Executed
1513 Duke of Suffolk	Leading surviving Yorkist claimant to the throne – accused of treason	Executed
1521 Duke of Buckingham	England's most powerful noble-man. Had a claim to the throne if Henry died – accused of treason	Executed

How did Henry VIII run his government? At first he ruled like his father. S. T. Bindoff, a historian, tells us that:

J *Down to 1509 one man alone holds the stage, the king; after 1509 there will be two, a king and a minister, and at times the minister may appear greater than the king.*

? ? ? ? ? ? ? ? ? ? ?

1 Look carefully at pictures **D** and **E**. Close the book, and then describe as fully as you can scene **E**.

2 Compare account **B** with portrait **C**. Deal with each item of clothing in turn – cap, doublet, tights, collar and cloak.

3 If you had met Henry VIII in 1515, say what you think he would have looked like, how clever and religious he was, how he passed his days at court, his wars, how he treated his enemies and how he ran the country.

4 How much trust can you put on the *evidence* on these pages? Draw up a table like the one below with your ideas.

Source	What kind	How reliable is it?
	(e.g. painting, photograph, eye-witness account)	

WOLSEY

The date is 28th November 1530. The place is a bedroom in Leicester Abbey. The king's prisoner, Cardinal Wolsey, lies dying. From 1512 he had been Henry VIII's chief minister and run the country for him. By Wolsey's side was his servant, George Cavendish, who later wrote about the Cardinal. Cavendish gives us important clues as to why and how Wolsey gained power, how he ruled, and why he fell into disgrace. Wolsey was the son of a butcher and trained to be a priest. By 1512 he had been Henry VIII's chaplain (almoner) for three years. Cavendish tells us:

A *The king was young and lusty; disposed all to mirth and pleasure, and to follow his desires and wishes. He did not care at all to work on the busy affairs of the government. This the almoner (Wolsey) saw very well. Therefore he took on himself to remove the weight and trouble of business from the king.*

Wolsey took great care to keep Henry in touch with everything that went on. Why did Henry trust him to run the country? Cavendish talks

C

1514	Bishop of Lincoln
	Bishop of Tournai
	Archbishop of York
1515	Cardinal
1518	Bishop of Bath and Wells
	Papal Legate – Head of the English Church
1521	Abbot of St. Albans – England's richest monastery
1523	Bishop of Durham
1528	Bishop of Winchester

about the 1512-14 war with France and Scotland (see pages 10-11).

B *The king judged no man to have his wisdom and cleverness. He had a special gift of eloquence, . . . and was able to persuade and attract all men to his plans. . . . It chanced that war started between the realms of England and France. . . . The king decided . . . in his most royal person to invade his foreign enemies with a powerful army and to stop their haughty boasting.*

Therefore it was thought vital that this royal plan should be quickly carried out and provided with every kind of thing it needed. The king thought no other man was able to

plan and work as hard as his beloved almoner. He handed over the whole affair to him. . . . Though it seemed to others very difficult, yet he took over the full weight of this business. . . . All was arranged in good order and carried out successfully. All kinds of food, supplies and other needs of so noble a voyage and powerful an army were organised.

The speed and skill with which Wolsey carried out Henry's wishes meant that by 1514 he was in full charge of the government. This allowed him to become the greatest churchman in England. **C** gives an idea of the number of offices he held.

These posts gave him a huge income – some £50 000 a year. Much of this money he spent on building great palaces. Hampton Court is the most famous of these. As well as looking after home affairs, Wolsey ran Henry VIII's foreign policy. Henry wanted to be as great a king as the rulers of France and Spain. Wolsey worked non-stop to achieve this. In June 1520 he arranged a meeting between Henry VIII and Francis I of France. They met near Calais. With them they brought all their courtiers, who slept, feasted and danced in a large number of tents and marquees. The largest was painted and

woven in gold cloth. Wolsey saw to every detail – such as wine, stables, jousts and negotiations. The meeting is known as the "Field of Cloth of Gold". Can you think why? Wolsey even hoped in 1521 to become Pope himself. In 1522 Henry VIII joined Charles V, King of Spain and ruler of much of modern Holland and Germany, in a war against Francis I, King of France. The war ended in 1525 – with no gains for Henry or Wolsey.

By 1527 Wolsey had failed to achieve Henry's goals in foreign affairs. However, Wolsey still seemed to be in firm control of England. This was not so, for Henry VIII had fallen in love with a young court lady, Anne Boleyn. Henry wanted to marry her, and divorce Queen Catherine. She was now too old to have the son Henry wanted. Anne Boleyn was Wolsey's bitter enemy. Wolsey had stopped Anne from marrying a nobleman she loved. Therefore she was happy to back noblemen who plotted against Wolsey. Because Wolsey was unable to get Henry a divorce from his Queen, Anne and her backers got Henry VIII to remove him from power by 1528.

??????????????

1 **D** is a picture based on George Cavendish's drawing of Wolsey leaving Hampton Court. Answer these questions:
   a Which figure do you think is Wolsey?
   b What is he riding on? What does it signify?
   c What kind of men are at the front of his procession?
   d What are the figures carrying at the bottom of the picture?
   e Why are they carrying these objects?
   f What does the procession suggest about Wolsey?

2 What do evidence **A** suggest about Wolsey's relationship with Henry VIII; evidence **B** about how he ran the government; and evidence **C** about his role in the church?

3 **E** is an official portrait of Wolsey. What kind of impression of him do you think he wanted it to give?

13

HENRY AND ROME,
1527-40

How many members of your form are Protestants? Of these, how many belong to the Church of England? How many are Catholics? In what ways do Catholics and Protestants differ? When, why and how did the different churches grow up? Before 1520 everyone was a Catholic. After 1520 Protestants emerge in Europe. At court a number of Henry VIII's noblemen became Protestants. Their chance to. turn England into a Protestant country came from Wolsey's failure in helping Henry VIII to divorce Queen Catherine. The short play which follows aims to give you some idea of what went on. The play is set in a Shropshire monastery. You can read about monastic life in *The Middle Ages.*

Narrator: It is 26th January, 1540, at Wenlock Priory, Shropshire. The monks are packing their bags and getting ready to leave. Here is the head of the monastery, Prior John Bayley. Prior, what is happening?

John Bayley: This morning, three of King Henry's servants arrived to take over the buildings, treasures and lands of the monastery for the king. We knew they were coming — two days befor they *dissolved* Shrewsbury Abbey about 15 kilometres away.

Narrator: How dreadful! Will you be thrown out onto the streets, with nothing to live on?

John Bayley: Well, not really. We have all got large pensions from the king. I'm going to live as a priest in a local town.

Narrator: Why has King Henry VIII made up his mind to shut down the monasteries?

John Bayley: It's a long story. For years the public have said that the way the monasteries are run is a scandal. There are very few monks left — many priests despise us because we no longer follow the strict rule of St. Benedict. (See *The Middle Ages, page 56.*) Wenlock is a typical monastery. In 1522 there was a big enquiry into our affairs. It said:

The rule of continuous silence must be kept more strictly.

There must be no contact with women. They are forbidden *absolutely* to go into the cloisters.

Gambling on games of cards, marbles and chess is forbidden.

The Prior must not indulge in rich and extravagant living, with a large household.

Narrator: It sounds as though it was a bit like holiday camp. To be fair, you were made Prior to clear up the mess at Wenlock — typical of corruption in many monasteries. But this was not the reason Henry VIII took over the monasteries and attacked the Pope. In 1521 wasn't Henry very pleased when the Pope appointed him Fidei Defensor — Defender of the Faith?

John Bayley: That's perfectly true. If you look at one of today's coins, you will see the initials *F D* on it. The real trouble started when the church got mixed up in politics. By 1527 Henry VIII was desperate to have a son, and Queen Catherine was getting too old to have any more children. Normally Henry would have been able to divorce — kings always could. First he had to get permission from the Pope. The Pope was willing but he could not grant Henry's wish. The Pope was the prisoner of Charles V — and he was Queen Catherine's nephew. This meant that Henry could not marry a young court lady, Anne Boleyn, who could bear him a male heir.

Narrator: Couldn't Wolsey and Henry fix up something with the Pope? After all, Wolsey was a very cunning and experienced diplomat.

John Bayley: They tried every trick in the book. The trouble was that in 1525 Wolsey had double-crossed Charles V at the end of the war with France. Charles' aunt, Catherine, refused to consider a divorce. She was as stubborn as a mule. The Pope even sent a cardinal to England in 1528 to try and get Catherine to agree to divorce. This is what Catherine told Henry at the enquiry:

Catherine of Aragon: I have been your wife these twenty years and more. By me you have had several children. When you married me, I take God to be my judge, I was a true maiden. Whether that is true or not, I leave to your conscience. If there is any just case that you can allege against me, either of dishonesty or an unlawful act, to put me from you, I am content to depart, to my shame and rebuke. And if there be none, then I pray you to let me have justice at your hands.

John Bayley: She then stormed out of the enquiry. Henry called her back — but she wouldn't come. He still hoped that the Pope would give him a divorce, but Charles V refused to let him. Aunt Catherine kept writing him pleading letters. In 1527 Charles had conquered Italy — which explains why the Pope was his prisoner.

Narrator: Henry was stuck. Madly in love with Anne Boleyn, he had no son and heir, and his wife refused to give him up.

John Bayley: That's right. Henry was in a fix. Finally he decided to make himself head of the English church instead of the Pope. He needed to get Parliament to back him. In 1533 it passed *The Act of Appeals*:

> *This realm of England is an Empire, and so has been accepted in the world, governed by one Supreme Head and King, unto whom a body politic (the country's people) be bound and owe next to God a general and humble obedience.*

Narrator: In other words, Henry VIII had broken with the Roman Church so that he could go ahead and marry Anne Boleyn. It also meant that he could seize the Catholic church's property — which meant nationalizing the monasteries.

John Bayley: Quite. In 1534 Anne and Henry married. Soon Anne had a baby — Princess Elizabeth. IN 1536 Henry decided to seize all the smaller monasteries. Wenlock escaped this time, as it was worth £401 a year. Remember, the Roman church owned about a quarter of England's land — it was the biggest landholder.

Narrator: Wasn't there a nasty rebellion in 1536 in northern England against Henry's attack on the Catholic church?

John Bayley: Yes, the Pilgrimage of Grace. Henry was terrified of rebellions. He ordered that those who took part . . .

Henry VIII: . . . should be hung up on trees, chopped into quarters, and their heads and quarters set up in every town, great and small, and in all other such places.

Narrator: Charming! So Henry was determined to be head of his own church. Changes in religion began — England was turning Protestant. In 1537 he introduced a Bible in English, to replace the Latin version. By 1539 he was ready to take over the big monasteries.

John Bayley: He made sure that anybody who stood in his way was ruined. His old and best friend, and chief judge, Thomas More, refused to accept him instead of the Pope as head of the English church. More was arrested, tried and sentenced to death. In 1535 he was taken from the tower, as William Roper, his son-in-law, tells us:

William Roper: Master Lieutenant brought him out of the Tower, and from there to the place of execution. When going up to the scaffold, he was so weak that he was ready to fall. He said merrily to master Lieutenant:

Sir Thomas More: I pray you, Master Lieutenant, see me safe up. For my coming down, let me shift for myself.

Narrator: So Henry was head of the church, and owned all of its buildings, treasures and lands. All opponents had been crushed. This explains why these three men have come to take over Wenlock Abbey. Further changes and reforms — the *Reformation* — occurred in the English church. We can look at these along with John Bayley on pages 22-23.

?????????????????????????????

1 What do these words mean? **a** Protestant; **b** Catholic; **c** Dissolution; **d** Fidei Defensor.

2 What were: **a** The Act of Appeals; **b** The Pilgrimage of Grace.

3 Who were: **a** Thomas More; **b** Charles V; **c** Catherine of Aragon; **d** Anne Boleyn; **e** John Bayley.

4 What happened in 1521; 1525; 1527; 1533; 1534; 1536; 1539; 1540?

5 Imagine you were a monk at Wenlock monastery on 26 January 1540. Write a letter to your father, saying what has happened to the monastery, and why.

6 Use the information on these pages to explain why and how the English Church had broken away from the Roman Catholic Church by 1540.

THOMAS CROMWELL

A is a portrait of Thomas Cromwell in 1535. He was Henry VIII's chief minister from 1532-40. What thoughts about Cromwell do you think the painter wants you to have? Who was Thomas Cromwell? What was he like? What ideas did he have? How did he run the government? G. R. Elton is the world's leading expert on Thomas Cromwell. Elton writes of the young Cromwell:

> **B** *Thomas Cromwell was born about the year 1485, the son of a clothworker of Putney in Surrey, who like others of his trade, also kept an ale house. His early life is very obscure. . . . However, it would appear that in his teens he got into sufficient trouble to leave the country for a while, and he made his way through the Netherlands into Italy where he allegedly served as a soldier. . . . He then turned to trade, serving a Venetian merchant.*

Cromwell came back to England, married and in about 1516 began to work for Wolsey (see pages 12-13). By 1519 he was one of Wolsey's advisers, and had also begun to be a great success as a lawyer. Through the 1520s he worked closely with Wolsey as his secretary, and when Wolsey fell from power he got a job

C	**Thomas Cromwell's Reforms**
1533	Act of Parliament to make Henry VIII head of the English church.
1534	Acts of Parliament to make clergy obey Henry VIII.
1535	Survey of monasteries' wealth and lands – *Valor Ecclesiasticus*
1536-40	Complete reform of the way in which the government ran. Council reform, reform of tax collection.
1536	Dissolution of small monasteries.
1537-40	Religious reforms, including introduction of the *Bible* in English.
1539	Dissolution of the large monasteries.

with the king. Soon Henry VIII realised he was as good in government as Wolsey. From 1532 Cromwell ran Henry VIII's government for him. Table **C** gives an idea of how he changed things. So great was Cromwell's impact on the government, that G. R. Elton wrote a book on it, called *The Tudor Revolution in Government*.

Cromwell's letters and papers give us clues about how he ruled. The brief extracts **D – F** deal with an Irish rising, guide lines for priests and Cromwell's hope that Henry VIII would marry Anne of Cleves, a protestant princess from Europe. On 17 March 1539 Cromwell wrote a long letter to Henry VIII. Part of it said:

> **D** *I understand from Ireland that your rebels Desmond, Brien, O'Neil and O'Donell do much combine and practise together. I think it a miracle of the arrival of the Irish monk, which the weather drove here. There were four ships at their departure for Scotland a fortnight before. . . . By tempest three of them drowned in the other's sight, whereby this monk was driven to your grace's land by the wind. Whereto of all places in the world he was most loth to arrive. It shall be a great hindrance to the said Irish rebels purposes and practices when they themselves know their messenger is so interrupted. We can as yet get to the heart of his knowledge, whereby I am . . . tomorrow to go to the Tower and see him placed in the rack and by torture compelled to confess the truth. . . .*

In September 1538 Cromwell laid down clear orders to England's clergy. These commands included:

> **E** *. . . you shall provide (before Christmas) . . . , one book of the Holy Bible of the largest volume in English, and the same set up in some convenient place within the said church . . .*
>
> *. . . that such images as you know in any of your cures (parishes) to be so abused with pilgrimage or offerings of anything made thereunto, you shall for avoiding of that most detestable offence of Idolatry forthwith take down and destroy. And shall allow from henceforth no candles, tapers or images of wax to be set before any image or picture. But only the light that commonly goes across the church . . .*

> *. . . that you, and every parson, vicar or curate within this diocese shall for every church keep one book or register wherein you shall write the day and year of every wedding, christening and burying made within your parish for your time, and so every man succeeding you likewise.*

On 14th January 1539 Cromwell penned lengthy orders for Christopher Mount, who was going to negotiate a treaty with the Duke of Cleves. Part of his orders said:

> **F** *Further, the said Christopher Mount shall diligently but secretly enquire of the beauty and qualities of the Lady (Anne), oldest daughter to the Duke of Cleves, as well what shape, stature, proportion and complexion she is of, as her learning, activity, heavier and honest qualities, and if the said Christopher Mount shall hear that she is such as might be liked by his majesty.*

Christopher Mount's report and a portrait led Henry VIII to agree to marry Anne. When she came to England, Henry loathed her on first sight. He was so angry with Thomas Cromwell for getting him to wed her, that he sided with Thomas' enemies at court. They had him arrested, and executed soon after, in July 1540.

? ? ? ? ? ? ? ? ? ? ? ?

1 Say what portrait **A** tells us about Thomas Cromwell.

2 Using evidence **B**, what skills do you think Thomas Cromwell had which helped him when he became Henry VIII's chief minister?

3 What does evidence **D – F** tell us about how Cromwell:
   a dealt with the Irish; **b** treated prisoners; **c** wanted religion to be taught; **d** wished priests to keep records; **e** carried out foreign policy.

4 Why did G. R. Elton write that Cromwell carried out a 'Revolution in Government'?

5 Compare Thomas Cromwell as the head of the government with the Prime Minister today.

HENRY VIII: 1533-47

A

Look carefully at portrait **A** of Henry VIII towards the end of his reign. What kind of person do you think it shows? Already you have some ideas about the king from pages 10-17. These pages examine EVIDENCE about other sides of his character.

How did he treat his chief ministers?
What happened to Wolsey, Sir Thomas More and Cromwell give some ideas. Earlier in Henry's reign, when he had been friendly towards Sir Thomas More, Sir Thomas told William Roper, his son-in-law:

B . . . if my head could win him (Henry VIII) a castle in France (for then there was war between us) it should not fail to go.

After Sir Thomas' death in 1535, Roper informs us:

C Intelligence thereof came to the Emperor Charles. Whereupon he sent for Sir Thomas Elyot, our ambassador, and said to him: "My Lord Ambassador, we understand that the king, your master, has put his faithful servant and grave, wise councillor, Sir Thomas More to death". . . (Elyot did not know).
"Well", said the Emperor, "it is too true. And this we will say, that if we had been master of such a servant, of whose doings ourself have had these many years no small experience, we would rather have lost the best city of our lands than have lost such a worthy councillor."

What did Henry VIII think of Cromwell's death? G. R. Elton tells us:

D Less than a year after the event Henry knew well enough that he had been tricked into killing "the most faithful servant he had ever had."

How did he treat his wives? Table **E** shows what happened to them.

E

Name	Married	Children	Fate
Catherine of Aragon	1509	Mary, 1516	Divorced, 23 May 1533. Died 1536
Anne Boleyn	28 May 1533	Elizabeth, 1534	Accused of Adultery. Executed, 18 May 1536
Jane Seymour	30 May 1536	Edward, 1537	Died 1537
Anne of Cleves	1540		Divorced, 10 July 1540. Outlived Henry
Catherine Howard	9 August 1540		Accused of adultery. Executed, 1542
Catherine Parr	1543		Outlived Henry.

F

After portrait **F** was sent to Henry, Anne of Cleves arrived from Europe in 1540 to marry Henry. On their first meeting Henry was horrified − she was much uglier than the picture had made out. Forced to marry Anne, Henry soon fell in love with a young court lady, Catherine Howard. Henry divorced Anne and married Catherine. In September 1540 the French Ambassador in London wrote:

G *The King is so in love with Catherine Howard that he does everything for her, and is with her much more than the others (his old wives).*

Catherine was unfaithful to Henry, for she soon tired of the old, fat and sick King. Henry found out, was furious and had her tried and beheaded in 1542. In 1543 he married a devout court lady, Catherine Parr, who out-lived him.

How did he govern and make war? From 1540 Henry VIII ran the government himself.

No longer did he rely on a chief minister. As at the start of his reign, Henry was keen to fight wars. From 1542-6 he fought both France and Scotland − the old enemies. Little was gained, and in 1544 he led an army of 40 000 men to France. Henry could not walk, as an ulcer was rotting his leg. He directed his army from a litter, and wrote home to Catherine Parr about the siege of a town:

H *. . . our supply of powder is not come from Flanders as we thought it would. Within two or three days we hope to have it here, and shortly afterwards we hope to sent you some good news. And yet, for the time being, we have done something important. For we have won, without any loss of men, the strongest part of the town which is the outwork of the castle.*

Henry gained nothing from the wars when they ended in 1546. With only Prince Edward as a male heir, Henry was still afraid of what would happen when he died. Just before his death in 1547 he had the Earl of Surrey beheaded because he had hinted that his family might have a claim to the throne.

1 Henry VIII relied upon portrait **F** when he decided to marry Anne of Cleves. How does it make her appear? Describe her looks in detail.

2 Use the evidence on these pages, and on pages 12-15 to draw cartoons to show what happened to Henry's wives.

3 If, in 1547, you had been a Spanish ambassador at the court of Henry VIII what would you have said in a letter home about: **a** his marriages; **b** how he treated his ministers; **c** how he reigned after 1540; **d** his religious ideas.

4 Can we trust the evidence we have used to try and find out about Henry VIII? Draw up a list, saying what each piece of evidence is, and how reliable you think it is.

THE BOY KING: EDWARD VI

Do you keep a diary, or write stories about how you pass your time? Throughout his reign King Edward VI (1547-53) kept a diary. His schoolteachers made him begin it in 1547, when he was nine. It tells us much about him. Because he was so young, a council of noblemen ran the country for him. Its head was his uncle, the Duke of Somerset. Edward's diary tells us what the Council talked about, and also some of his adventures, such as a day out on the Thames:

> **A** *I went to Deptford . . . where before supper I saw certain men stand on the end of a boat without holding anything and run at one another until one was thrown in the water. . . . After supper a castle was built upon a great barge on the Thames, with three walls and a watchtower in the middle. Mr. Winter was the captain, with forty or fifty other soldiers in yellow and black. By the castle was a galley, yellow in colour, with men and ammunition to defend the castle. Then arrived four small pinnaces (small boats), their men handsomely dressed in white, which intended to attack the castle. First they drove away the yellow galley, and afterwards with clods (of earth), fireworks, burning sticks, darts and grenades, they attacked the castle, and broke down the outer wall. They pushed back the defenders into the inner part, who then rushed out and drove away the pinnaces, sinking one of them. Out of this, all the men in it (being more than twenty) leaped into the Thames.*

What kind of schoolboy was Edward? An eyewitness tells us that Edward:

> **B** *When only a child, could speak many languages. . . . He wrote both Latin and French, and some Greek, Italian and Spanish.*

C is a portrait of him. A bishop who knew him well wrote that he collected:

> **D** *A copy of every sermon that he hears,*

C

> *and most carefully requires an account of them after dinner from those who study with him. Many of the boys and youths who are his companions in study are well and faithfully instructed in the fear of God and good learning.*

Edward was brought up to be a strict Protestant — the religion of his mother and of his uncle the Protector, the Duke of Somerset.

1 Pretend you were a soldier on the pinnace that sank. Make up a story of what happened that day. Use these ideas to help you — sight of the king; building the castle; dressing for the fight; four boats; approach castle; weapons; the fight; the pinnace sinks; rescue.

2 How would you feel if you were king or queen? At some time in his reign, Edward was your age. Read carefully through the page above, and pages 21, 22 and 23. Say what thoughts and feelings you might have, if faced with Edward's problems in 1547.

EDWARD VI AND TRADE

The news often says how British *exports* — what we sell abroad — are doing. The clothes you wear, the food you eat, the wages your family earns, *all* depend upon how well we can sell what we make to foreign countries. In Tudor times much of England's wealth also relied on trade. Most important was the export of wool cloth. Map **A** shows where most of it was sent, and table **B** how the cloth trade did from 1450-1600. Up to 1560 it grew very quickly, although there were problems. In March 1552 Edward VI was worried that England's main wool fleet had again arrived late at its most important European market, Antwerp. This meant its cloth sold at a low price. What was to be done? Edward wanted to set up an international market at Southampton, to replace Antwerp. The young king wrote:

C *It is easier for the Spaniards, Bretons, Gascons, Lombards, Genoese, Normans and Italians to come to Southampton than to go to Antwerp. . . . Southampton is a better port than Antwerp. . . . The Flemings* (of Antwerp) *by giving privileges lured men to make a market there, making very few goods* (of their own). *We shall do it* (set up a market) *more easily, having cloth, tin, sea coal, lead, bell metal and other goods.*

Edward's Council refused to back his plan, and Antwerp stayed the centre of the wool trade.

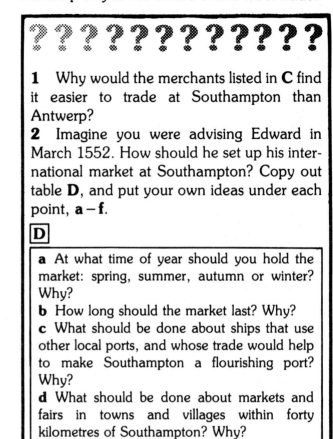

????????????

1 Why would the merchants listed in **C** find it easier to trade at Southampton than Antwerp?
2 Imagine you were advising Edward in March 1552. How should he set up his international market at Southampton? Copy out table **D**, and put your own ideas under each point, **a** – **f**.

D

a At what time of year should you hold the market: spring, summer, autumn or winter? Why?
b How long should the market last? Why?
c What should be done about ships that use other local ports, and whose trade would help to make Southampton a flourishing port? Why?
d What should be done about markets and fairs in towns and villages within forty kilometres of Southampton? Why?
e What plans should you make to get Southampton ready for the fleet of foreign ships which will come to the market? What about: the harbour; docks for boat repairs; hotels; streets; warehouses; local government; courts for disputes. Why?
f Any other ideas?

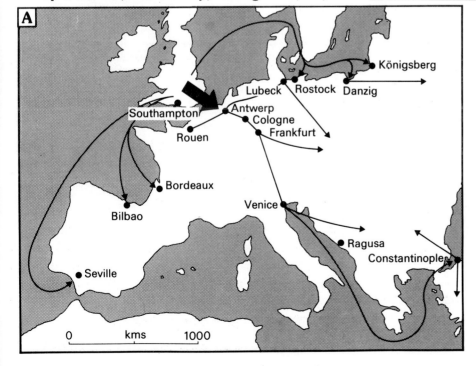

A

B

Value of Wool Trade	
1450-59	100
1460-69	98
1470-79	unknown
1480-89	130
1490-99	128
1500-09	158
1510-19	168
1520-29	155
1530-39	180
1540-49	240

EDWARD, THE PROTESTANT KING

A Catholic Customs of Henry VIII's Time

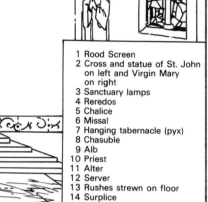

1 Rood Screen
2 Cross and statue of St. John on left and Virgin Mary on right
3 Sanctuary lamps
4 Reredos
5 Chalice
6 Missal
7 Hanging tabernacle (pyx)
8 Chasuble
9 Alb
10 Priest
11 Alter
12 Server
13 Rushes strewn on floor
14 Surplice
15 Statue of the Virgin
16 Wall painting

B New Protestant Ways

1 Plain glass in window
2 Wall tablets
3 Book of Common Prayer at north end of table. The priest now stands there at communion service
4 Ordinary bread
5 Flagon for wine
6 White linen cloth
7 Table
8 Pulpit for preaching
9 Royal coat-of-arms
10 Priest
11 Scarf of black silk
12 Surplice
13 'Eagle' lectern for Bible

Thus saith the Lord: Thou shalt not... (Ten COMMANDMENTS)

Our Father

Narrator: John, we last met on 26th January, 1540, when you were about to leave Wenlock Priory. (See pages 14-15.) It is now July 1553. Here in Shrewsbury we have just heard that Edward VI has died. If Princess Mary, Edward's sister, becomes queen, what changes in religion made by Henry VIII and Edward will she have to tackle?

John Bayley: Well, as you know she is a Catholic — and under Edward VI everyone had to become a Protestant.

Narrator: What did that mean?

John Bayley: Protestantism spread from the teachings of Martin Luther, a German, after 1517. He said that the Pope should no longer be in charge of religion and tell us how to worship. Instead we should all rely on the words of the Bible and pray directly to God. Priests' sermons would help us to understand the Bible.

Edward agreed with Luther. Henry VIII's Council had made a start when it dissolved the monasteries, introduced a Bible written in English and church services in English and made Henry VIII head of the English church.

The first thing Edward VI's Council (see page 24) did was to order priests to wear plain clothes and to destroy paintings, carvings and statues in their churches. In 1547 a Shrewsbury man wrote in his diary:

> **C** *This year images were ordered to be taken down and thrown out of churches, beads and processions forbidden, and priests allowed to marry in England.*
>
> *The picture of our Lady from St Mary's in Shrewsbury, the picture of Mary Magdalene and the picture of St Chad from Saint Chad's Church in the same town were all three burned in the market place there. . . .*

John Bayley: Many churches had their insides whitewashed, which covered up the bright and cheerful old wall paintings.

Narrator: How very dull. So these changes, this *Reformation*, affected every church in the country?

John Bayley: Yes — **B** and **C** give you an idea how. In 1549 Edward's Council made another big change. Our Shrewsbury writer tells us:

> **D** *This year was set forth in England by authority of Parliament a book made for the uniformity of Common Prayer and the administration of Sacraments in English, and the Mass was clean abolished.*

The old Roman religion was now gone. (See **E**.) The kind of worship you have today in Church of England services had been established. Not everyone was happy — there were bloody risings in Cornwall, Devon and Somerset. These were put down, and many of the rebels were hanged.

? ? ? ? ? ? ? ? ? ? ?

1 *Either* draw a picture of a church's inside in 1553 to show the changes which had happened in the previous twenty years *or* make out a list of what those changes were and why they had happened.

2 Describe what religious changes there had been since 1530. To help you, look at pages 14-15.

23

SOMERSET AND NORTHUMBERLAND

A shows the fate of Edward VI's uncle, the Duke of Somerset, in 1552. When Edward became king five years earlier, Somerset had been the head of his government with the title *Lord Protector*. How Somerset ran the government upset many of Edward VI's Council. Their leader was the Earl of Warwick. The split in the Council led to Somerset's disgrace in 1549. Edward VI's diary tells us of the crisis:

> **B** *In the mean season, because there was a rumour that I was dead, I passed through London. After that they (the people) rose in Oxfordshire, Devonshire, Norfolk and Yorkshire.*

The most serious rebellion was in Norfolk. The Earl of Warwick crushed this rising, and captured its leader Robert Ket. Edward's diary now records:

> **C** *The Council, about nineteen of them, were gathered in London, thinking to meet with the Lord Protector and to make him put right some of his mistakes. He fearing his state, caused the Secretary (of the King) in my name to be sent to the Lords to know for what cause they gathered their powers together and, if they meant to talk with him (to say) they should come in a peaceful manner. The next morning, being the 6th of*

October, and Saturday, he commanded the armour to be brought down out of the armoury of Hampton Court, about 500 sets, to arm both his and my men, the gates of the house to be fortified, and people to be raised. Many people came to the house. That night, with all the people, at nine or ten o'clock at night, I went to Windsor, and there was watch and guard kept every night. The Lords sat in . . . London . . .

Somerset soon realised that he had no backers. Edward tells us that the Council wrote to him, complaining of:

> **D** *his faults, ambition, vainglory, entering into rash wars in mine youth, negligently looking on Newhaven, enriching of himself of my treasure, following his own opinion, and doing all by his own authority . . .*

The councillors then arrested Somerset, and imprisoned him in the Tower of London. The Earl of Warwick became head of the Council. In 1551 he was made Duke of Northumberland. In 1552 he had his old rival, the Duke of Somerset, beheaded.

???????????????

1 Draw three cartoons which show the events described in **B**, **C** and **D**.

2 Tell the story of what happened on 6th October 1549, as if you had been with Edward VI. Mention: news of the situation in the morning; Somerset's plans to fight; the move to Windsor; rumours.

3 Use this information and what you can discover in other books to explain what the Council's letter meant when it talked of all Somerset's faults. Deal with each point in turn, e.g. **a** ambition; **b** vainglory; **c** entering into rash wars.

LADY JANE GREY

Pictures **A** and **B** show the tragic story of a young court lady, Jane Grey, in 1553. What do they suggest happened to her? **C** is a list of events which led up to her death.

Historians think that Edward VI and the Duke of Northumberland were behind the scheme to put Lady Jane Grey on the throne. Edward

Lady Jane Proclaimed Queen

knew in early 1553 that he was dying from tuberculosis. He was desperate to keep England a Protestant country, and realised that his half-sister Mary would restore Catholicism. The best plan seemed to be to make Lady Jane Grey Queen. On Edward's death the plot was bungled.

Lady Jane Beheaded in y^e Tower

C

21 May	Guildford Dudley, the Duke of Northumberland's oldest son, marries Lady Jane Grey, a second cousin of Edward VI and claimant to the throne.
June	Edward VI's will leaves the throne to Lady Jane Grey. Judges and Councillors forced to accept this will.
3 July	Princess Mary flees to safety in Suffolk, a Catholic area.
6 July	Edward VI dies.
10 July	Lady Jane Grey proclaimed as Queen. Mary raises an army and marches on London.
20 July	Northumberland tries to raise a force to fight Mary. Everyone deserts him. He surrenders to Mary at Cambridge without a fight.
3 August	Mary enters London in triumph. Lady Jane Grey, Guildford Dudley and Northumberland imprisoned in the tower, tried and executed.

?? ?? ?? ?? ?? ?? ?? ?? ?? ?? ??

1 *Either* describe in detail scenes **A** and **B** or draw four cartoons to show the story of Lady Jane Grey.

2 As if you were Lady Jane Grey, upon the eve of your death, write the story of your attempt to gain the throne in the form of a letter to your sister.

3 Treason! If you had been advising Northumberland in May 1553, how would you have suggested he seized power? Use points **a – g** to make out a plan of how you would have acted, and the reasons for your decisions.

   a Seize Mary, and place her in the Tower of London.

   b Call Parliament, and get it to declare Mary is no longer heir to the throne.

   c Get the councillors and judges to publicly witness the will of Edward VI which makes Lady Jane Grey Queen.

   d Arrest all the leading Catholic noblemen and pro-Catholic bishops.

   e Raise or hire a large army.

   f Call a curfew in London.

   g Conceal the death of Edward VI until you are ready to strike.

BLOODY QUEEN MARY

Do you or your friends have nicknames? If so, what are they? How did you get them?

Mary, Queen of England from 1553-58, had a nickname – Bloody Queen Mary. Do you know why?

Let us look at some evidence – **A** – **F** – about her reign to see how she got her nickname, and if she deserved it.

A is an extract from the diary of Thomas Wriothesley, a courtier. Lady Jane Grey's short rule had just ended. The news spread like wildfire through London that Mary was Queen:

> **A** *All the people and citizens of the City of London for such joyful news made great and many fires through all the streets and lanes within the said City. With the setting out of tables in the streets and feasting also, with all the bells ringing in every parish*

church in London till ten of the clock at night, the inestimable joy and rejoicings of the people cannot be reported.

A Catholic wrote **B** after he saw Thomas Cranmer, Edward VI's Archbishop of Canterbury, burned at the stake. Queen Mary insisted that everyone became a Roman Catholic. Many Protestants fled abroad. Those who stayed were punished – and this often meant that they were burned to death. Cranmer:

> **B** *Coming to the stake with a cheerful look and a willing mind, he put off his clothes quickly, and stood upright in his shirt. . . . The fire now lapping round him he stretched out his right hand and thrust it into the flame.*

C is an extract from the diary of Henry Machyn, a London merchant, written on 18 May 1555.

C *The same day of May four men from Exeter were tried at St Paul's in the morning and they were convicted of heresy, and the four were convicted to be burned.*

D shows what the burnings that Machyn wrote about were like. Henry Machyn described many such deaths in Smithfield, London's market place. **D** is from John Foxe's *Book of Martyrs*, written in 1563, about Protestants whom Catholics had killed. Foxe's book became a best-seller, and reprinted many times.

Map **E** shows the number of people burned for heresy in the reign of Mary , 1553-58.

F is a coin celebrating the marriage in July 1554 of Queen Mary and Philip of Spain, heir to the Spanish throne. Philip and his Spaniards were very unpopular. When Mary said she was going to marry Philip, a rising broke out in Kent under Sir Thomas Wyatt, who marched to the gates of London. Mary was in great danger. Her troops in London managed to defeat Wyatt and he was captured and executed. Hundreds of his supporters were hanged. Mary's marriage was a failure, for she had no children. In 1557 Mary helped Philip fight France. During the war the French captured Calais, the last English stronghold in their country.

Although Mary had restored the Catholic religion, in 1558 she was an old, sick and dying Queen. The heir to the throne was Princess Elizabeth – Anne Boleyn's daughter. Elizabeth was a Protestant, and as Mary lay dying she probably knew that her plans to make England a Catholic country would die with her.

F

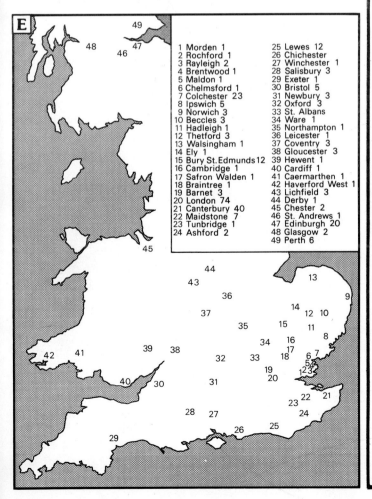

E

1 Morden 1	25 Lewes 12
2 Rochford 1	26 Chichester
3 Rayleigh 2	27 Winchester 1
4 Brentwood 1	28 Salisbury 3
5 Maldon 1	29 Exeter 1
6 Chelmsford 1	30 Bristol 5
7 Colchester 23	31 Newbury 3
8 Ipswich 5	32 Oxford 3
9 Norwich 3	33 St. Albans
10 Beccles 3	34 Ware 1
11 Hadleigh 1	35 Northampton 1
12 Thetford 3	36 Leicester 1
13 Walsingham 1	37 Coventry 3
14 Ely 1	38 Gloucester 3
15 Bury St.Edmunds 12	39 Hewent 1
16 Cambridge 1	40 Cardiff 1
17 Safron Walden 1	41 Caermarthen 1
18 Braintree 1	42 Haverford West 1
19 Barnet 3	43 Lichfield 3
20 London 74	44 Derby 1
21 Canterbury 40	45 Chester 2
22 Maidstone 7	46 St. Andrews 1
23 Tunbridge 1	47 Edinburgh 20
24 Ashford 2	48 Glasgow 2
	49 Perth 6

???????????

1 Judge whether Mary deserves her nickname 'Bloody Queen Mary', by looking at a piece of evidence.

Evidence	Does she deserve her nickname?
A	
B	
C	
D	
E	
F	

2 What does **F** suggest about how Mary thought of her husband, King Philip of Spain?

3 Describe scene **D**. Who do you think are being burned and why?

4a Why did Queen Mary and her Catholic followers burn Protestants for heresy?

b What does **E** suggest about the extent of Mary's persecution of Protestants?

c Why do you think Wyatt rebelled?

QUEEN ELIZABETH I

On 17th November 1558 the London merchant Henry Machyn wrote in his diary:

A *. . . in the afternoon all the church in London did ring, and at night people made bonfires and set out tables in the street, and did eat, drink and make merry for the new Queen Elizabeth.*

What was the new Queen like? Her school-master said:

B *Nobody's understanding can be quicker than hers, no memory better. French and Italian she speaks like English, Latin with fluency. . . . Also, she talks Greek with me.*

Before Elizabeth became Queen, she had been accused of plotting to overthrow her older sister, Queen Mary. Elizabeth wrote letter **C** to Mary, ending:

D *And as for the copy of the letter sent to the French King, I pray God confound me eternally if ever I sent him word, message, token or letter by any means, and to this truth I will stand in till my death. . . . I humbly crave but only one word of answer from yourself.*

When Elizabeth was crowned as Queen, an artist painted **E**. At court young noblemen flattered the beautiful young queen. The Scottish Ambassador wrote about a meeting with Elizabeth:

F *In her desk was a parcel on which was written, "my lord's picture". I held the candle, and pressed to see that picture so named. She was loath to let me see it, but at length my pressing gave me sight of it. I found it to be the Earl of Leicester's picture.*

The twenty-five year old queen faced many dangers, and had to make up her mind about them straight away. What were her problems?

Religion What religion should the country have? There were three choices, **a – c**:

a Henry VIII's idea. Henry kept on worshipping like a Catholic, but refused to accept that the Pope in Rome was in charge of the Church in England. By 1547 neither devout Catholics nor Protestants were happy with this system.

b Edward VI's Protestantism. The Protestant way of worshipping became the country's official religion under Edward VI (see pages 22-23). Catholics refused to accept it.

c Mary's Catholicism. Mary had restored the Catholic faith – with disastrous results (see pages 26-27). An added danger of keeping the Catholic religion was the landowners' fear that they would lose the lands they had gained from the monasteries since 1540.

Marriage Who should she marry? If she died, it seemed that civil war would break out, as there was no obvious heir to the throne. Should she:

d Marry an English nobleman – possibly her favourite, the handsome young Earl of Leicester. This could split the court and lead to a rebellion of jealous nobles.

e Marry the French king. Although England and France were at war, this would give England a strong ally. But it might mean French control over England. The French king was a devout Catholic.

f Marry the Spanish king – Philip II, Mary's ex-husband. Elizabeth would then face the same problems as Mary, although Spain would be a useful ally against France.

g Marry a German Protestant prince. If Elizabeth decided to support the Protestant religion, it would be useful to have an ally in Europe.

h Remain unmarried and keep rivals for her hand ever hopeful. This would mean that she could keep on ruling England without taking orders from her husband. The danger was that she needed an heir to avoid a civil war on her death.

Foreign policy England was at war with France, as a result of Queen Mary's marriage with Philip of Spain. What should Elizabeth do? Should she:

j Make peace with France and accept the loss of Calais.

k Make peace and then ally with France.

l Make peace and keep the Spanish alliance.

m Make peace and try to be neutral. The problem here was that the Pope had refused to accept her as queen. He would recognise her as ruler of England if she had French or Spanish support. Also, this would mean that Catholics in England would not plot to over-throw her.

n Ally with a German Protestant power. The danger with this was that the French might use their base in Scotland to try and over-throw Elizabeth. The Scottish queen, Mary Queen of Scots, was 16 years old. The ruler of Scotland was her mother, a French princess.

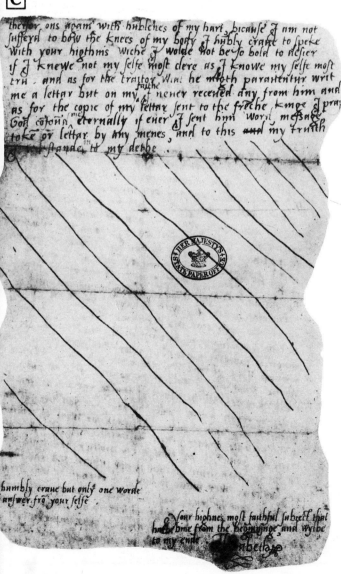

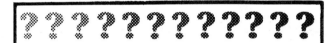

1 Use the *evidence* on this page, and anything else you can find out, to say what kind of queen you think Elizabeth was when she came to the throne in 1558. Mention:
 a Her looks – *evidence* **E**.
 b Her education – *evidence* **B**
 c Her court life – *evidence* **F** and pages 30-31.
 d Her problems – *evidence* **C** and **D**, and points **a – m**.

2 Look at **C** and **D**. Why did Elizabeth:
 a Ask for "one word of answer" in reply to her letter.
 b Mention the "copy" of the letter to the French king?
 c Draw lines across the unused page?
 d Write a postscript at the bottom of the page?
What does this suggest about her political skill?

3 For each area of policy, religion, marriage and foreign policy, choose *one* of the plans listed, and say why you would prefer Elizabeth to have followed it in 1588 in preference to the alternatives suggested.

QUEEN ELIZABETH'S COURT

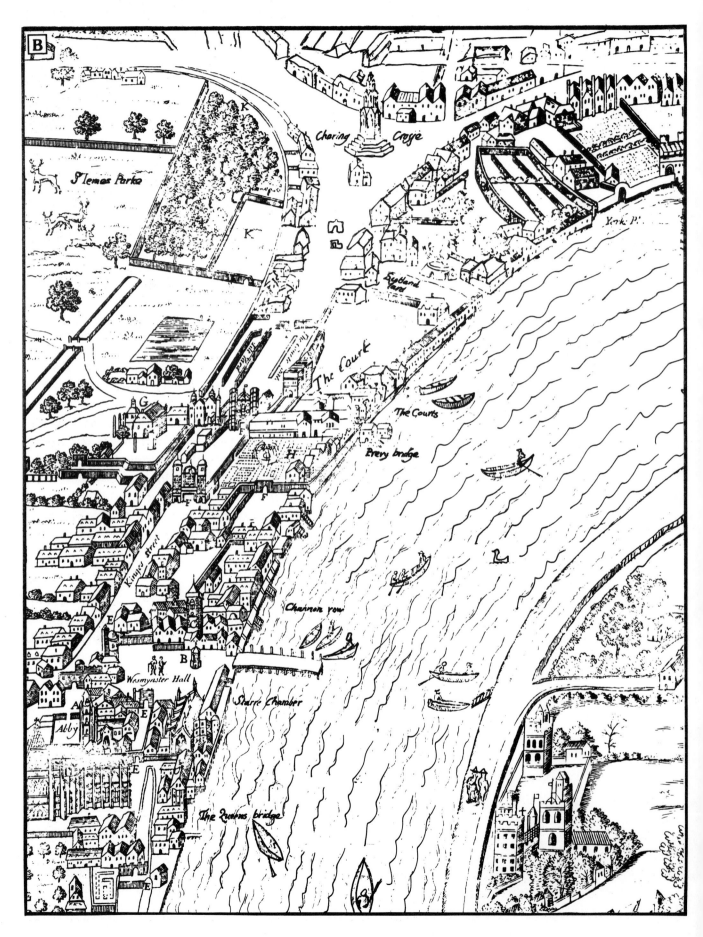

Have you seen pictures of, or visited, Buckingham Palace, the home of our queen? What do you think court life is like today? How has it changed from the time of Queen Elizabeth I (1558-1603)? The diary of a German tourist, Thomas Platter, in 1599, gives us some clues:

> **A** *September 20th. After our meal, I and my party visited the Royal Palace in London, where the Queen (when in London) holds her court. It is called Whitehall. . . . This palace is sited above the bridge (London Bridge) on the River Thames, on to which back lovely gardens. Before the entrance to the palace is the tilt-yard, at its centre a barrier about a horse's height, on either side of which the competitors joust. Next to this yard is the park, where we saw a number of fallow deer, many white ones amongst them.*

B is a view of Whitehall from above, drawn in 1570. Thomas Platter carried on his story:

> **C** *We climbed the steps into the Palace. The floor of the first chamber . . . was strewn with rush-matting and the walls hung with fine pictures and tapestries. From this room we entered a chamber built over the water, hung all round with emblems and mottoes.*

They were shown round:

> **D** *. . . this fine, but unfortified, Palace, which contains the Queen's wardrobe, where she keeps her clothes and jewels, which are worth a huge amount of money. Besides other curiosities I saw a huge whale rib . . . Likewise a delightful garden. The rooms contain many beautifully worked tapestries, almost as if they were painted.*

> *We were also shown the Queen's library, containing many books written in her own hand in Latin, very clearly indeed. For she can speak this tongue as well as French, Italian and Spanish. In some of the apartments I saw small organs and virginals, which she plays, daintily made couches, also numerous clocks, cleverly built in all sizes. I saw too in this Palace an Indian bed, with an Indian bedcover, and an Indian table . . .*

Court life could be gay, with balls, plays, feasts and picnics – like the one in **E**. Queen Elizabeth ran the government from Whitehall – as does the Prime Minister today from 10, Downing Street.

??????????????????????????

1 *Either* use **A–C** to draw a plan of Whitehall Palace to show: the tilt yard, the deer park, the gardens and the Palace buildings *or* imagine that you were a member of Thomas Platter's party. Write a story about your day at the Palace. Mention: your arrival (by boat); where the palace is; the tilt yard; the deer park; the royal rooms.

2 Look *carefully* at **E**. Describe in *detail* the scene shown.

3 What does the *evidence* on this page tell you about what kind of queen Elizabeth was?

4 How different was Queen Elizabeth's court from that of our Queen?

ELIZABETH AND PARLIAMENT

A shows Queen Elizabeth at the House of Lords. Members of the House of Commons are also present, standing at the foot of the picture. Queen Elizabeth is listening to a speech from the Speaker of the House of Commons, who is standing in the middle of the members. In his speech to the Queen he asks her to give the members of the House of Commons two rights or privileges. These are freedom of speech and freedom from arrest. This meant that they could say what they liked in the House of Commons, and would not be arrested for anything they said. Can you think why this was very important?

Elizabeth's parliaments helped her rule the country by passing Acts of Parliament to raise taxes and solve problems. Acts of Parliament dealt with matters such as the country's religion and how the poor should be looked after. **B** is a list of when Parliament met, and the main Acts it passed and things it talked about or debated.

B	
1559	January – May. First Parliament. Act of Supremacy. Act of Religious Uniformity. Treason Act.
1563	January. Second Parliament. Act for Relief of the Poor. Act for controlling craftsmen. (Continued to meet occasionally until January 1567.)
1571	April – May. Third Parliament. Act against the Pope and Roman Catholics.
1572	May – April. Fourth Parliament.
1585	November – September. Fifth Parliament.
1586	October – March. Sixth Parliament.
1589	February – March. Seventh Parliament.
1593	February – April. Eighth Parliament. Act against Catholics living in England. Great debate on government's attempt to raise extra taxes.
1597	October – February. Ninth Parliament. Act for Relief of the Poor. Act for punishing Rogues and Vagabonds. Act for building Workhouses and Hospitals.
1601	October – December. Tenth Parliament. Debate on government monopolies. Act for Relief of the Poor.

In Elizabeth's 44 year reign Parliament had thirteen sessions and met for 140 weeks.

??????????????

1 Use table **B** to say how important you think the Elizabethan House of Commons was, and what it did.

2 Use history books to answer the following questions:

    a How many M.P.s were there in Elizabeth's Parliament?

    b How were they chosen?

    c Where were their seats?

    d How many members were there of the House of Lords?

    e How have the jobs of the following changed since the time of Elizabeth: The Black Rod; The Speaker; the Lord Chancellor; an M.P.?

THE CATHOLIC THREAT

A

In religion Queen Elizabeth backed the Protestants. With Parliament's support she set up the Church of England, with herself at its head. Today the Church of England is run in the same way. Catholics hated Elizabeth's changes. In 1569 in the north of England they rebelled – The Rising of the North. Elizabeth's army scattered the rebels. Many were hanged. In 1570 the Pope excommunicated Elizabeth, and said that Catholics need no longer obey her. Elizabeth faced many Catholic plots to remove her from the throne, and in return she and her ministers hunted out Catholics who opposed her. From 1570 Catholic priests were outlaws. One, Father William Weston, **A**, wrote that when he was staying with a Catholic family:

B . . . the house was surrounded by a large mob . . . the servant rushed up to my room – I was still there – and warned me of the danger. She made me come downstairs at once and showed me a hiding place. . . . Meantime the heretics had already made their way into the house and were examining the remoter parts. From my cave-like hide I could follow their movements by the noise and uproar they raised. Step by step they drew closer, and when they entered my room, the sight of my books was an added incentive to their search. In that room also was a secret passage for which they demanded the key, and as they opened the door giving on to it, they were standing immediately above my head. I could hear practically every word they said. "Here! Look!", they called out, "A chalice! And a missal!" . . . Then they demanded a hammer and other tools, to break through the wall and panelling. They were certain now that I could not be far away.

While I was worrying, one of the men . . . shouted out, "Why waste time getting hammers and hatchets? There's not enough space for a man. Look at the corners. You can see where everything leads. There can't be a hiding place here". They took the fellow's word for it, and the party left off its search.

. . . The whole of that day I lay in hiding, and the night and day following it as well, almost till sunset. The hiding place was dark, dank and cold, and so narrow that I was forced to stand the entire time. Also I had to stay completely quiet, without coughing or making the smallest noise. If they failed to find me, I thought they would surround the house and cut off my escape. During those long hours not a servant came to open the door, and this con-firmed my fears that the enemy was still in the house. But something had to be done, otherwise the hiding place would have become my tomb while I was yet alive.

I climbed the ladder. For a long time I strained my ears to catch the noise of voices or passing footsteps. But not a sound reached me. Nothing at all, though I waited for a long time. I was at the top of the ladder, and now I pressed my shoulders against the trap-door which had been shut down on me from the other side. With a great effort, and with prayers to help me, I was just able to push it open. But I was in great fear: if I used too much force, the rung of the ladder might have snapped and give way under my feet. Then it would have been all over. The fall was huge, and I would certainly have been killed.

???????????

1 Father Weston was able to escape. Pretend what it might have been like to have been him. In your own words say what thoughts and feelings might have gone through his mind when:

   a He realised that the Protestants had come to arrest him.

   b He entered the hiding-hole.

   c He heard the searchers getting ready to break in.

   d He had spent a day in the hole.

   e He decided to escape.

   f He escaped by standing on the ladder.

   g He emerged from the darkness.

MARY QUEEN OF SCOTS

In 1559 Scotland was one of Queen Elizabeth's biggest problems. Scotland's ruler, Mary Queen of Scots, was wife of the French king. During a war between France and England, Scotland would pose a major threat. Also, the Catholic Mary was Elizabeth's heir (see **A**). To Catholics who did not recognise the Protestant Elizabeth, Mary was England's lawful queen.

Scotland's Protestants feared Mary and the French as much as Queen Elizabeth did. The Scottish Protestants rose against Mary in 1559. What was Elizabeth to do? When the French sent troops to Scotland in January 1560 Elizabeth struck. In February she allied with the Scottish Protestants, and in March an English army marched to their aid. The French were beaten, and by the Treaty of Edinburgh the Scottish leaders made a lasting agreement with Elizabeth. Mary Queen of Scots was an exile in France, and Queen Elizabeth's Scottish problems seemed over.

In December 1560 Mary's husband, the French king, died — and Mary decided to return to Scotland. Her complex adventures are told below in the form of a short play. Again the leading character is John Bayley (see pages 14-15). The play is set in Bridgnorth, the Shropshire town where John Bayley lived as a priest after the Dissolution of the Monasteries.

Narrator: It is February 1587. John, have you heard the news? Mary Queen of Scots has been executed at Fotheringay, Northamptonshire, on the orders of Queen Elizabeth.

John Bayley: Praise be to God! The Scottish vixen has finally come to her deserved end. This realm of England is now free from her foul plots and attempts to destroy our Protestant religion and remove our blessed Queen.

Narrator: Why has Queen Elizabeth killed Mary? And why has Mary been Elizabeth's prisoner for some eighteen years?

John Bayley: It's a long story. As a girl Mary was brought up in France as a Catholic. She was married to the French King — who died in 1560. Mary's enemies were now France's rulers. So Mary returned to Scotland as its Queen in 1561 — but to a *Protestant* country. Its Protestant lords refused to obey her. Troubles began in 1565, when she married Lord Darnley, a young and foolish English nobleman, **B**.

Mary soon hated her husband. In turn Darnley loathed Mary's close friend and secretary, David Riccio. Riccio had other enemies at Mary's court. A group of Scottish nobles persuaded Darnley to let them break into the Queen's private rooms. One of them, Lord Ruthven, tells us that while Darnley held the screaming Queen:

> *The remainder of the gentlemen took David out of the Queen's chamber and slew him at the Queen's outer door. David was thrown down stairs. The King's (Darnley's) dagger was found sticking in his side.*

Narrator: So the young and beautiful Queen had seen her husband murder her close friend. Was it now that she fell in love with a Scottish Lord — the Earl of Bothwell?

John Bayley: Yes, this was a terrible mistake. Bothwell was a tough and ambitious soldier. He thought he could run Scotland. By this time Darnley had caught a revolting disease from one of his lovers, and was going blind. Bothwell wanted to get rid of Darnley — and blew up his house. Darnley

A Mary Stuart's Claim to the Throne

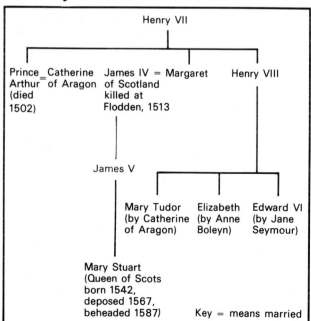

Henry VII

Prince Arthur (died 1502) = Catherine of Aragon

James IV of Scotland killed at Flodden, 1513 = Margaret

Henry VIII

James V

Mary Tudor (by Catherine of Aragon) | Elizabeth (by Anne Boleyn) | Edward VI (by Jane Seymour)

Mary Stuart (Queen of Scots born 1542, deposed 1567, beheaded 1587)

Key = means married

may have suspected danger, for he was found lying strangled in the grounds.

Narrator: But wait. We aren't certain Bothwell had Darnley killed — the evidence wouldn't stand up in court.

John Bayley: Ah, but Mary now married Bothwell — which made him the new King of Scotland. His fellow nobles weren't going to stand for that — you can guess what they said about Darnley's death. They rebelled against Mary and put her in prison. Bothwell fled to Denmark, whose king captured him and held him to ransom. But Bothwell went mad and died. The Protestant lords proclaimed Mary's baby son (born 1566) King James VI of Scotland.

Narrator: Mary escaped to England in 1567, where she threw herself on Elizabeth's mercy. But how was Elizabeth going to treat Mary — the Catholic heir to Elizabeth's throne? We know what happened under the last Catholic queen (see pages 28-29). Very difficult.

John Bayley: To put it mildly. Elizabeth kept Mary a prisoner. Catholics in England looked to Mary as their leader. In 1569, the great Catholic landowners in the North of England rebelled against Elizabeth. Their leader was the Duke of Norfolk. The Earls of Northumberland and Westmorland raised an army to fight Elizabeth. This force was beaten, and many of the rebels were hung. Elizabeth thought Mary had plotted against her — but nothing could be proved. Elizabeth pardoned Norfolk, Northumberland and Westmorland — but they were to plot against her once more.

In 1570 the Pope excommunicated Queen Elizabeth — which meant that many Catholics recognised Mary as their true queen. Elizabeth was really in danger.

Narrator: You mean that Catholics could plot to murder Elizabeth?

John Bayley: Yes, and in 1571 their leaders took part in a conspiracy — the Ridolfi Plot — to remove Elizabeth from the throne and make Mary queen. Elizabeth was ready for them. Her minister Walsingham had a team of spies at work. In 1572 the Duke of Norfolk was beheaded for his treasonable part in the Ridolfi Plot. Mary had still not been ensnared.

Narrator: Well, how was she brought to the block?

John Bayley: The Babington Plot did the trick. Mary smuggled messages in beer barrels out of her prison to Anthony Babington, a Catholic who planned to murder Elizabeth. Walsingham was opening the beer barrels, and reading Mary's messages.

Narrator: So Elizabeth had proof at last that Mary was trying to murder her.

John Bayley: So it seemed — although Mary denied everything at her trial. She had all the Tudor family brains, and ran rings around her accusers. You see, her accusers couldn't produce anything in Mary's own handwriting. So she denied everything.

Narrator: But her judges found her guilty all the same. Elizabeth was virtually forced to have Mary's head chopped off.

John Bayley: Yes. On the news of Mary's conviction, the Shrewsbury chronicler wrote in his diary:

C *For joy thereof the bailiffs and aldermen (the town council)* caused bonfires and bells to ring, and assembled themselves in their best costumes and banqueted and rejoiced at the same, praising God with triumph and the sound of trumpets.

1 Quiz time. We can hold a quiz, using the information on these pages.
What happened in: 1559; January 1560; December 1560; 1561; 1565; 1569; 1571; 1572; 1587?
Who were: The Duke of Norfolk; Mary Queen of Scots; Walsingham; Anthony Babington?

2 Write a letter as if you were a Protestant in 1587 in favour of Mary's execution. You are living in the town of Shrewsbury, and your brother was burned as a heretic in Queen Mary's reign.

ELIZABETH AND SPAIN – THE ARMADA

Philip II, King of Spain, was furious. That morning, 20th April 1587, he had heard that Sir Francis Drake had burnt thirty royal warships in an attack on Cadiz harbour. This was the final insult. For years Elizabeth's sea captains – pirates to a man – had been plundering Spanish ships and even attacking their settlements in South America. (See pages 62-3.) In 1585 Elizabeth had allied with the Protestant rebels in the Spanish province of the Netherlands – modern Holland and Belgium. The rebels wanted to set up their own Protestant country free from Catholic Spanish rule. In February 1587 Elizabeth had executed the Catholic Mary Queen of Scots. (See pages 34-5.) Now came this attack on Cadiz.

Philip decided to build up a fleet, an Armada, to invade England. This would remove the Protestant heretic Elizabeth from her throne and make England Catholic again. An Armada would finish the work that his wife Mary, Queen of England, had started from 1553-58.

By July 1588 the Armada – about 110 warships and 40 supply ships – was ready to sail. Facing it was an English fleet of about 100. The fighting vessels in both fleets were about the same size, **A**. In late July and early August the Spanish sailed up the Channel in crescent formation, fighting off English attacks. The

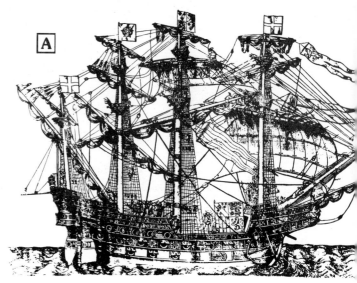

Armada anchored off Calais, and the English sent fireships against it. These were old vessels stuffed with pitch and tar to set fire to the Spaniards' boats. The Armada fled from Calais and scattered. On 8th August in the Battle of Gravelines, the English warships attacked the scattered Armada. The Captain of one of the vessels wrote later:

B *The enemy opened heavy cannon fire on our flagship at seven o'clock in the morning, which carried on for nine hours. So tremendous was the fire that over 200 balls struck the sails and hull of the flagship on the starboard side, killing and wounding many men, disabling and dismounting guns and destroying much rigging. The holes made in the hull . . . caused such a great leak that two divers had as much as they could do to stop them with tar and lead plates, working all day. The galleon San Felipe of Portugal was surrounded by seventeen of the enemy's ships, which directed heavy fire on both sides and on her stern. The enemy approached so close that muskets and pistols on the galleon were brought into action, killing many enemy men on the enemy ships. The enemy did not dare, however, to come to close quarters, but kept up a hot cannon fire from a distance, smashing the rudder, breaking the foremast and killing over two hundred men in the galleon.*

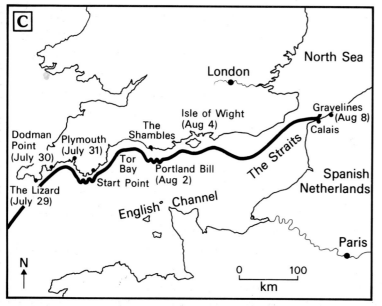

C shows the route of the Armada up to the Battle of Gravelines. Gravelines was a defeat for the Armada. It had failed to get its army to England. On their way back to Spain many ships were wrecked in storms. Only sixty-nine out of one hundred and forty got home safely.

A major historian, G. Mattingly, who wrote a book on the Armada, tells us that the first account of the Armada was by Petruccio Ubaldini. When this was translated into English in 1590 Robert Adams drew charts based on the text. He was surveyor of the Queen's Buildings as well as being interested in naval affairs and could have had advice from some Elizabethan captains. **D** is based on his work.

???????????????????????????????????????

1 Look carefully at **A** and **D**. What would it have been like to have fought against ship **A** – the flagship of the English fleet? How would you have felt if you had commanded a ship in action, **D**? Use the evidence on these pages to write an account of the attack on the *San Felipe* from her captain's viewpoint. Use these ideas to help you: Cadiz; fireships; cut anchor; dawn; Gravelines; scattered fleet; English warships; closing; prepare guns; broadsides; surrounded; chaos; masts; rigging; muskets; cries; blood; escape.

2 After the Battle of Gravelines the battered but intact Armada reformed. What should its captains do?

a Try to sail back down the channel to Spain. They would face the British Navy, supplied with food and ammunition again, and not as badly knocked about as the Armada.

b try and get to the Spanish Netherlands. They would have to wait for the Duke of Parma to get the Spanish army ready, before trying to cross the Channel. To do this they would have to defeat the English navy.

c Go north, and try to reach Spain by sailing around Scotland. The ships are leaking, food is short, many men are wounded, and typhus, a deadly disease, is spreading through the fleet. Scotland, under its Protestant rulers, is an enemy power. The English rule Ireland.

As the *San Felipe*'s Captain, put these plans into your order of choice, and argue in favour of your first decision.

3 The *evidence*. What we know about the Armada is based on evidence from the time (primary sources) and on what historians tell us (secondary sources).

a Which of **A**, **B** and **D** are primary and secondary sources?

b How reliable do you think **D** is?

QUEEN ELIZABETH AND THE POOR

Queen Elizabeth faced a major and growing problem — that of the poor. **A** and **B** show two sides of Tudor poverty. Why were there so many poor people — the old, the sick, and out of work men and women during her reign? Pages 48-50 give us some clues. Increase in the numbers of the poor arose from these four reasons:

a The closing of the monasteries.
b Changes in farming, with the enclosure of the fields and more sheep farming.
c An increase in population.
d The end of war, with a cut in the size of the army and navy.

Gangs of poor roamed the countryside, moving from village to village. They were called sturdy beggars. What kinds of problems do you think they caused?

How did the Tudors deal with the poor? **C** shows one answer. Elizabeth and her Parliament tried to solve the problem by Acts of Parliament. The most important of these were passed in 1598 and 1601. They set up the *Tudor Poor Law*, **D**. This lasted for over two hundred and thirty years.

Be it enacted, that the churchwardens of every parish and four well-off house-owners . . . shall be called overseers of the poor. . . . They shall . . . set to work the children of all parents who shall not . . . be thought able to keep and support their children, and also all persons who, married or unmarried, having no means to maintain them, use no ordinary and daily trade of life to get their living by . . .

THE END OF THE REIGN

By 1603 Queen Elizabeth was an old, sad woman who ruled alone. In 1598 Lord Burghley had died. For forty years he had been her chief minister, and had helped run all her affairs. Elizabeth had hoped that a young lord, the Earl of Essex, would take Burghley's place. But Essex soon showed that he was not good enough for the job. He failed to carry out his tasks. She had sent him to Ireland to crush a rising. Essex's troops could not defeat the rebels. In 1599 Essex came back to England, although Elizabeth wanted him to stay in Ireland. He hoped to become Elizabeth's favourite, and run the government for her. Instead of making him welcome, Elizabeth was very angry with him for failing in Ireland. Essex was in disgrace, and had no hope of gaining the posts which Burghley had held. In 1601 with the help of a group of soldiers he tried to seize power. The troops of Elizabeth stayed loyal. They captured Essex, who was put into the Tower of London. Elizabeth had him beheaded for treason. Sir John Harington was a close friend of Essex. In October 1601 he wrote a letter about the Queen, just after Essex's rising.

A . . . these troubles waste her much . . . . Every new message from the city (of London, where Essex had led his rebellion) does disturb her, and she frowns on all the ladies. I had a sharp message from her . . . namely thus, "Go tell that witty fellow, my godson, to get home: it is no season to fool it here." I like this as little as she does my knighthood (Essex had made him a knight, something only the Queen was allowed to do) so took to my boots and returned to the plough in bad weather. I must not say much, even by this trusty and sure messenger: but the many evil plots and designs have overcome all her highness' sweet temper. She walks much in her privy chamber, and stamps with her feet at ill news, and thrusts her rusty sword at times into the arras (curtains) in great rage.

In 1601 Elizabeth had big problems with the House of Commons. Its members hated paying heavy taxes to pay for the war in Ireland, and the struggle against Spain which had carried on since the Armada (see pages 36-7). Elizabeth's troubles remained throughout 1602, and she died in March 1603 (**B**). The new ruler was her distant cousin, James VI of Scotland, who became James I of England.

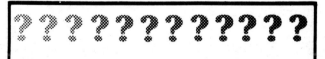

1 What *evidence* is there in **A** that Harington is:

    a a "witty fellow"?   **b** afraid?

2 Write out four different things which Harington tells us about the mood of the Queen. Use these pieces of evidence to say what idea Harington gives us of Elizabeth in 1601.

3 Why do you think Queen Elizabeth was "an old, sad woman who ruled alone" by 1603?

THE TUDOR VILLAGE

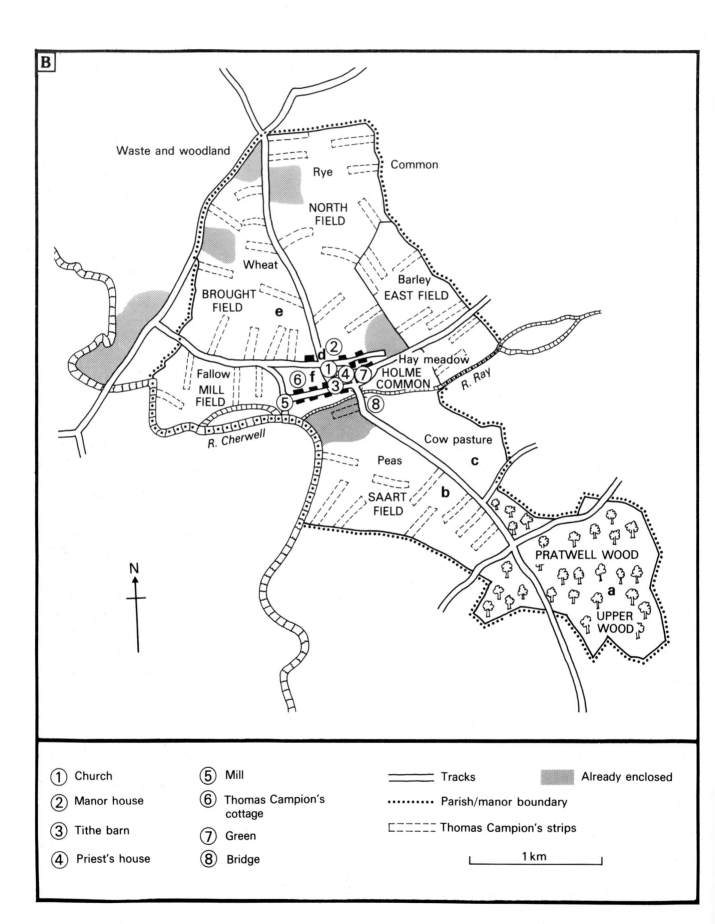

B

Waste and woodland

Common

Rye

NORTH FIELD

Wheat

Barley EAST FIELD

BROUGHT FIELD

e

② d

Hay meadow

Fallow MILL FIELD

⑥ f ① ④ ⑦ HOLME COMMON

③

⑤

⑧

R. Ray

R. Cherwell

Cow pasture

c

Peas

b

SAART FIELD

PRATWELL WOOD

a

UPPER WOOD

N

① Church	⑤ Mill	——— Tracks	▒ Already enclosed
② Manor house	⑥ Thomas Campion's cottage	·········· Parish/manor boundary	
③ Tithe barn	⑦ Green	⌐‒‒‒‒‒ Thomas Campion's strips	
④ Priest's house	⑧ Bridge	⊢——— 1 km ———⊣	

40

The date is 13th February 1587. The place is the church hall of the village of Islip. The villagers are at a meeting of the Manor Court. The Court settles quarrels between the villagers over questions such as: who owns land, who has the right to graze animals on the common, and who has been trying to fence in (enclose) part of the common land. The Court also punishes villagers who break minor laws, perhaps by gambling and working on the Lord's day — Sunday.

Among the forty villagers at the meeting of the Manor Court are these four people:

Sir Richard Warren, the Lord of the Manor, who owns three hundred and twenty-five acres of land. He is the Court's judge.
Thomas Campion, a yeoman who owns the same forty acres of land that his ancestor, Godric the villein, farmed in Norman times (see *The Normans*).
George Wader, the vicar, who farms eighty acres of glebe land belonging to the church.
Will Cock, a peasant, who rents ten acres from the vicar.

From the records of the Manor Court, its Court Roll, we learn that:

A *George Wader, John Fuller, Thomas Campion, Will Austryn, Will Fuller and Will Coke played illegal games. Each fined 4d. Margaret Sympton permitted illicit gambling in her house, playing for drinks. Fined 6d.*

About three hundred people live in the village. Its lands are split up into five open fields, common, the meadow, heath and woodland — **B**. Two villagers are church wardens. They help run church affairs. Each year the villagers choose two *village constables*. They have to catch thieves; lock up tramps, called *sturdy beggars* (see page 38) who pass through the village; and stop fights. They keep their prisoners in the village goal. The Manor Court sentences them to the stock or to be whipped. If the crime is a serious one, they are sent for trial to the quarter sessions (see pages 42-43), the county's chief court.

During the week the villagers, adults and children, work in the fields, for there are no schools. Many men spend the evening in Margaret Sympton's ale house. Feasts and celebrations are held at certain times of the year. In spring, a Tudor writer tells us:

C *The Maypole . . . is covered with flowers and herbs, tied round with string from top to bottom, and sometimes painted in different colours . . . when it is set up, with handkerchiefs and flags streaming from the top, they strew the ground with straw. . . . Then they begin to banquet and feast, to leap and dance about it.*

At harvest time another Tudor writer tells us:

D *I happened to meet some country people celebrating their harvest home. Their last load of corn they crown with flowers, and have besides them a doll or idol, richly decorated . . . men and women, menservants and maidservants ride through the streets in the cart, shouting as loud as they can till they arrive at the barn.*

???????????????

1 Look at map **B**. What would you see in 1587 at the following places: **a b c d** (at Maytime); **e f** (at the end of the harvest)?

2 Imagine you were a Tudor writer interviewing the vicar. What might he tell you about: the Manor Court; the church wardens; the constables; Maytime; harvest festival?

3 Table **E** shows, out of a sample of one hundred families, how many gentlemen, priests, yeomen, peasants and craftsmen lived in a village like Islip. If there were fifty families in the village, how many of each kind would live there?

E

Occupations	%	Number of Families in Islip
Gentlemen	8	
Priests	2	
Yeomen	18	
Peasants	60	
Craftsmen	12	

THE JUSTICE OF THE PEACE: SIR RICHARD WARREN

Sir Richard owned the village's demesne farm, about three hundred and twenty five acres. A bailiff ran it for him. In 1570 Sir Richard pulled down his family's medieval manor house and built a more comfortable one, **A**. From 1570-1640 many country gentlemen built new houses.

A Tudor servant wrote of his work for a land-owner:

> **B** When your master intends to go to bed, see that you have a fire and candle ready. You must have clean water at night and in the morning. If your master lies in fresh sheets, air them at the fire. . . . Warm his night clothes and see his toilet is clean, help him off with his clothes and draw the curtains, make sure the fire and candles are safe, put out the dogs and shut the doors. . . . In the morning, if it be cold, make a fire, . . . bring him his warm petticoat with his doublet, and all his clothes clean and brushed, and his shoes cleaned. Help to dress him . . .

C shows what Tudor ladies and gentlemen wore.

Inventories list goods that people owned. They help us imagine the furniture in Sir Richard's bedroom.

> **D** Old tapestry work of images (pictures), seven pieces.
> An oak bedstead with an old mattress.
> A new featherbed with a bolster.
> A bedspread of green cloth with rabbits and fowls.
> A canopy of red damask cloth, and four curtains of red cloth.
> An old cupboard.

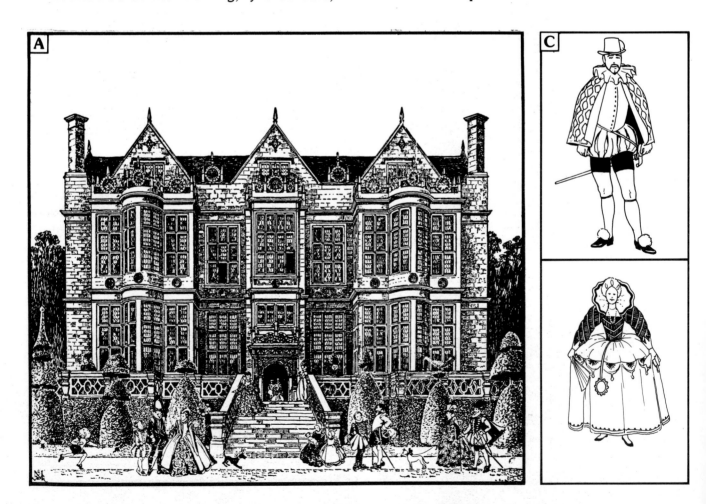

42

A cloth over the chimney with Mary and Gabriel.
A pair of tongs. A fire shovel.

E shows such a bedroom. Sir Richard was a Justice of the Peace — a local judge and civil servant appointed by the Queen. There were about forty JP's in the county. They ran all the government's local business — collected taxes, raised troops and announced government plans. Two or three times a year they met at quarter sessions in the county town to try serious crimes and decide how to run country business. Among Sir Richard's hobbies were hunting, shooting, cock-fighting and horse-racing.

?????????????????????????????

1 Looking at the *evidence*. What does picture **C** tell us? How is the man dressed?

Say what he is wearing on: his head; his upper body; his lower body; his legs.

What is he carrying around: his shoulders; his waist?

What does his dress, and what he is carrying, tell us about him? Can we trust what the picture tells us about a Tudor country gentleman?

Clue **E** shows a Tudor bedroom. Say what you think the scene is about.

2 Compare Sir Richard Warren's bedroom with your own, using clues **B**, **D**, and **E**.

3 If the servant in **B** showed you around Sir Richard's house, what might you see in the: parlour; main bedroom; hall?

4 List Sir Richard's jobs and then say who does them today.

THE YEOMAN: THOMAS CAMPION

On 14th February 1587, Thomas Campion wondered when to plough his one-acre plots in the open fields of the village. His family was the same as that of Godric the villein (see *The Normans* by Jon Nichol), and Thomas farmed Godric's land. **A**, **B**, **C** and **D** show some of Thomas' jobs in the farming year – very like those of Godric. Thomas is married to Alice. Alice helps Thomas on the farm. A Tudor writer described such a yeoman's wife:

E *It is a wife's job to winnow all types of corn, to make malt, to wash and wring, make hay, shear corn, and in time of need to help her husband fill the muck wain or dung cart, drive the plough, load hay, corn and such like. . . .*

Thomas and Alice lived in a cottage on the village green. **F** is a drawing of the inside of their cottage. **G** is an inventory (list) of the contents of a home like theirs:

G *Brass pot, 2 brass kettles, 2 old pans, 1 pair pot hooks.*
2 pewter dishes, 3 pewter platters, 2 saucers, several trencher plates, 6 trencher dishes.
8 wooden bowls, 12 trenchers, 12 trencher spoons.
2 candlesticks.
1 old feather bed, 1 flock bed, 1 mattress, 4 pairs of canvas sheets, 3 bedspreads, 1 blanket.
Tables and stools.
1 cart, 1 waggon, 4 horse collars, 4 pairs cart traces, 1 pair of harrows, 1 pair of plough traces, 1 plough.

At meal times Alice got ready, *"Bread, beer and beef, yeoman's food . . . full dishes, whole bellyfulls."*

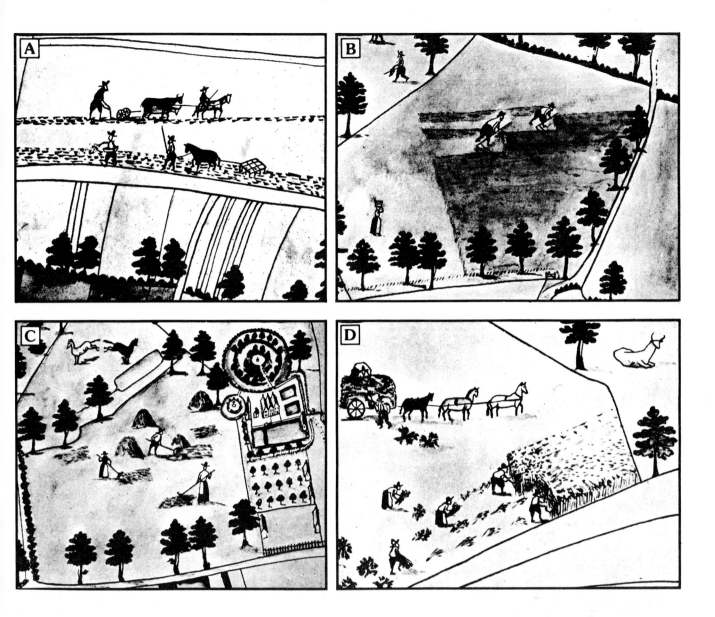

1 Work out your answers to this questionnaire about Thomas and Alice. Use the clues on this page, and those on page 40 for help.

a How many acres of land did Thomas own?

b What jobs did Alice do?

c What were: winnowing; making malt; a muck wain; an acre; a trencher; a harrow?

d At what times of the year would Thomas do the jobs shown in pictures **A**, **B**, **C** and **D**?

e Tell in your own words what is happening in each picture.

f How many of the objects in list **G** can you recognise in picture **F**?

g Each open field grew one crop a year. Next year it would grow a different crop. Every *fourth* year the field would be fallow – that is, grow nothing. How many acres of the following would Thomas grow in this year? **i** peas in Saart Field; **ii** barley in East Field; **iii** rye in North Field; **iv** wheat in Brought Field? Which field was fallow?

2 Imagine you walked around Thomas' farm in *July*. Describe what you would see at the following points: Upper Wood; Saart Field; cow pasture; Holme Commons; points 1-8 in the village; North Field; Brought Field; Fallow Field; enclosed lands.

3 Write a diary of a day in the life of Alice during the Spring ploughing.

PEASANT AND PARSON

William Cock worked on Thomas Campion's farm. William was the youngest son of a yeoman, and had no land of his own. On the common he had built a hut:

A *Walls of earth, low thatched roof, few rooms, no wood or glass windows, scarcely a chimney, other than a hole in the wall to let out smoke.*

Jane, his wife, found life very hard. A peasant woman like her told an interviewer that:

B *When she was young she was fair haired, and neither fat nor lean, but very slender in the waist. . . . She was very poor, and had to labour for her living. In a day she said she could reap as much as any man, and was paid as good a wage. At thirty she married, and had fifteen children, ten sons and five daughters.*

On Sundays William and Jane went to the local church. Its vicar, George Wader, was a Protestant, and had married. **C** shows a Tudor parson preaching. He happily accepted the changes that Queen Elizabeth made – she turned the clock back to the time of King Edward VI. (See pages 22-23). George Wader made a living from his own farm and from the *tithe*. Each villager had to pay a tenth (the tithe) of what he grew or made to the church – a kind of income tax.

George Wader lived and worked alongside the rest of the villagers of Islip. During the week he spent most of his time making sure his land was well farmed. He was like a well-off yeoman, and had two poor peasants to help him plough, sow and reap, and look after his animals. In the evenings he liked to leave his wife and family, and go to the ale house. One day he and some friends got drunk, and the records of the manor court tell us that he had to pay a fine.

????????????

1 If you were doing a survey of Tudor peasants, what answers might William Cock give to the following questions?

  a How many acres of land did he own?
  b What were the walls and roof of his hut made from?
  c Did it have a chimney, a glass or wood window?
  d How did he make a living?
  e Was he married?
  f If so, how many children?
  g How did he dress?

2 Do you think the village parson, George Wader, was happy to be a Protestant and not a Catholic?

WITCHCRAFT

"Murder, Murder!" cried George Wader, parish priest, as he held his dead wife in his arms. "Jane Cock, that witch, the devil's daughter, did this." In 1582 George gave evidence at Jane's trial for witchcraft. This is how he said the trouble started.

A *About summer twelve-month, he being in London, his wife had a duck sitting on certain eggs under a cherry tree in a hedge. And when the said duck had hatched, his wife did suspect one Jane Cock, a loose woman and a common prostitute, of having stolen her ducklings. His wife went to Jane Cock and accused her, and all too soundly told her off. But she could get no news of her ducklings, and so came home, and was very angry against the said Jane.*

Other things went wrong for George's wife. In the same summer, according to George, he:

B *. . . went to the parsonage, and there he gathered plums. And the said Jane Cock then came to the hedge, and said to him, "I pray you give me some plums, sir." And he said to her, "I am glad you are here, you vile prostitute!", and said, "I think you have bewitched my wife, and, as truly as God does live, if I see that she is troubled any more as she has been, I will not leave a stone unturned, and seek to have you hanged" . . . he told her different things she had bewitched, such as geese and hogs.*

Just before Christmas, George's wife felt very ill. She said to George two days before she died:

C *"Husband, . . . I am now utterly consumed by yonder wicked creature" . . . two days after she departed out of this world . . . repeating these words, "Oh Jane Cock. Jane Cock. She has consumed me!"*

1 **D** is a Tudor picture of witchcraft. The Tudors believed that evil spirits lived in the bodies of birds and animals. Look at the picture, and say what you think the following show: **a**; **b**; **c**; **d**; **e**; **f**; **g**; **h**; **i**; **j**. Then write a story about the scene.

2 Guilty or not guilty? If you had to defend Jane Cock, what would you say about the charges against her?

Jane was lucky — but two other women tried with her for being witches were found guilty and hanged.

3 Look at the evidence above — the picture and the points against Jane Cock. Then say why you think people believed in witches.

4 **E** shows how the Tudors tried to find out if a woman was a witch. She will be the person in the sack. Can you think what the test might be?

47

ENCLOSURE

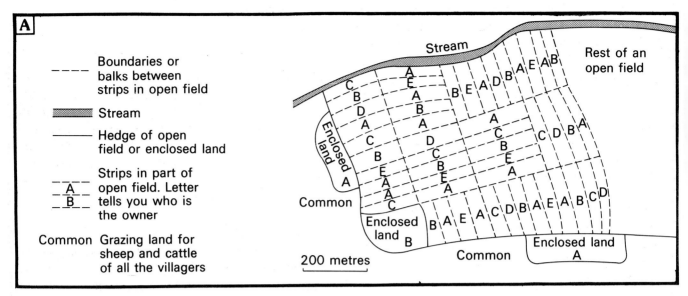

A

– – – –	Boundaries or balks between strips in open field
▓▓▓	Stream
————	Hedge of open field or enclosed land
A B	Strips in part of open field. Letter tells you who is the owner
Common	Grazing land for sheep and cattle of all the villagers

Stream

Rest of an open field

Enclosed land

Common

Enclosed land B

Common

Enclosed land A

200 metres

B

C

Map **A** shows part of one of Islip's open fields. The owners of the strips and enclosed land on the edge of the common are Sir Richard Warren, Thomas Campion, George Wader, John Fuller and William Fuller. They have agreed to meet in the parlour of Sir Richard's house to discuss whether they should enclose their lands to allow sheep and cattle grazing. **B** and **C** show an open field before and after enclosure. You represent *one* of these families. Table **D** tells you about the families concerned.

You have to decide whether your family is *for* or *against* enclosure. For the strips to be enclosed *all* the families who own land in that part of the field have to agree. Better-off landowners can offer to help poorer farmers with either money or land to get them to agree. Remember where your present strips and fields are when you consider the points below. Write out each point, and put your ideas down about them underneath each one.

a If land is enclosed, you can keep either sheep or cattle on it whose wool or meat can be sold for a large profit in the local town.
b You would not have to employ peasants to help work the land, as sheep or cattle only need one person to tend them.
c You would not have to worry so much about the weather if you keep animals. Crops can be easily ruined in storm or drought.
d At present your sheep and cattle have to mix with everyone else's on the common.

STRIPS A: Sir Richard Warren

For more about him, see pages 42-43. Sir Richard has heard a great deal from other JPs of the profits they have made from sheep and fattening cattle. His sons Robert and Michael have been educated at the local grammar school and Oxford, and favour new farming ideas. His daughters think money from sheep farming will let them buy some new court dresses.

STRIPS B: Thomas Campion

Thomas has seen the good money that is to be made from selling cattle in the county town. There is a thriving meat and leather trade. He feels that he could make money. But his sons John and James, and daughter Mary, are worried that there will be little work for them to do with the change from normal farming.

STRIPS C: George Wader

He was an old catholic who had married. He enjoys gambling and hunting, and is happy to please the squire. Sheep farming seems easy money. But his sons and daughters, Alfred, Thomas, Mary and Elizabeth are puritans. They oppose the enclosures

saying how much misery and poverty they have already caused. But it is George who takes the decisions.

STRIPS D: John Fuller

He only owns twenty acres. He is a poorer farmer, and is worried about what the changes might mean. Although he can see little money in enclosure for him, he and his three sons, Benjamin, Bernard, and Thomas, and daughters Prudence, Virtue and Margaret, all work on Sir Richard's demesne farm. They fear that they will be dismissed if they oppose the move to enclose this part of the village.

STRIPS E: William Fuller

He has thirty acres. A traditional old farmer, he can see little reason to change his ways. One of his worries is that his cousin William Cock lives on the common, in a squatter's hut. If the land is enclosed, William will be forced from his hovel with his wife and four children. They will have nowhere to live. William Fuller's sons, John, Adrian and Nigel think their father is a stick-in-the-mud, and hope to make some money from the changes in farming.

They catch horrible diseases they would avoid in enclosures.

e If the land is enclosed, peasants like William Cock will be evicted from their cottages, and will probably starve to death.

f For the small landowner there is no profit from sheep or cattle, as he can get more money for crops grown on the same land.

g There have been serious riots against enclosing, and the government has passed Acts of Parliament to make it illegal. **E** shows the amount of enclosure since 1455.

When your family has decided whether it is for or against enclosure, when asked tell the meeting, with your reasons. If you are against, the other landowners might try and get you to change your mind. As the decisions are announced, put a tick by those families in favour of enclosure, and a cross by those against.

If the families are in favour of enclosure, draw a map sharing out the land *fairly* between them. Each must have a *single plot* which reaches down to the stream and also has access to the *common*.

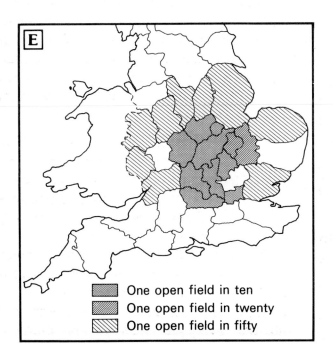

E
▨ One open field in ten
▧ One open field in twenty
▨ One open field in fifty

F Families	For Enclosure	Against Enclosure
Sir Richard Warren's		
Thomas Campion's		
George Wader's		
John Fuller's		
William Fuller's		

INFLATION

In the last five years, has the price of sweets and pencils gone up by 20%, 40%, 60%, 80%, or 100%? This *price rise* is called *inflation*.

The villagers of Islip and everyone else who lived in Tudor England also lived in an age of inflation. Prices rose because Tudor people had *much more money* — gold and silver — to buy *the same amount of goods*. This extra money came from South America. By 1550 the Spanish had defeated the Maya Empire in Mexico and the Incas in Peru. Both these empires were rich in gold and silver. The Spanish shipped this back to Spain.

The Spanish government turned the gold and silver into coins. They used the money to pay for the expenses of government. Most went to the army and navy. The Spanish King's forces were fighting in the Low Countries — modern Holland and Belgium. So much of the wealth of South America ended up there.

British merchants traded mainly with the Low Countries. Their chief port was Antwerp. They were paid in gold and silver coin. Also, the British government borrowed money in Antwerp. The bankers who lent the money got much of it from the King of Spain. They helped him to pay and run his forces in the Low Countries.

British merchants and the government spent the gold and silver from the Low Countries in Britain. Because there was more money but no more goods, prices rose.

How did inflation affect Tudor people? Let's look at three people — the Tudor gentleman, Sir Richard Warren, the yeoman, Thomas Campion, and the labourer, William Cock. To find about the prices rises impact, we can multiply their *income* and what they *spent* by how much *wages* and *prices* had risen. Use table **A** to do this. Where a gap has been left, multiply the figure in the left column by the number shown: eg × 2, or × 1½. This will give you each person's *income* and *expenditure* (what he spent) for each year.

?????????????

1 Make out the table, and fill in the gaps. Who do you think had done best out of inflation, and who was the worst off? Give reasons.

2 If you were Sir Richard Warren's steward in charge of his estate in 1600, how would you advise him to try and deal with inflation? What should he do with his:
   a lands — for ideas see pages 48-9
   b his family gold and silver plate
   c his house in London
   d industry — see pages 60-61
   e share in a raid on the Spanish Indies?
Write a letter to him, with your ideas.

A		1520	1550	1580	1600
William Cock (the labourer)	Week's wages	20d.	× 1½___	× 2½___	× 3 ___
	Week's food	15d.	× 2 ___	× 3 ___	× 4 ___
	Money left	___	___	___	___
Thomas Campion (the yeoman)	Income from land	£2	× 2 ___	× 3 ___	× 4 ___
	Pays in wages	£1	× 1½___	× 2½___	× 3 ___
	Profit	___	___	___	___
Sir Richard Warren (the gentleman)	Rent from estate	£20	× 1½___	× 2 ___	× 3 ___
	Cost of family house and life at court	£15	× 2 ___	× 3 ___	× 5 ___
	Money left	___	___	___	___

THE CHANGING VILLAGE

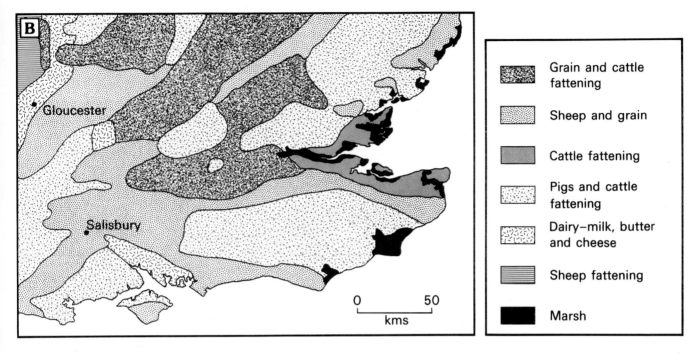

Legend:
- Grain and cattle fattening
- Sheep and grain
- Cattle fattening
- Pigs and cattle fattening
- Dairy—milk, butter and cheese
- Sheep fattening
- Marsh

Gloucester

Salisbury

0   50
kms

In villages like Islip during Queen Elizabeth's reign, life seems to have improved for the lord of the manor, the vicar and better-off peasants. William Harrison, a Tudor tourist, wrote in 1587:

A *There are old men yet dwelling in the village where I stay who have noted three things to be marvellously altered in England within their sound memory. . . .*

One is the multitude of chimneys lately erected (put up) whereas in their young days there were not above two or three, if so many, in most country towns. . . . But each one (houseowner) made his fire against a screen in the hall, where he dined and cooked his meat.

The second is the great, although not general, improvement in homes, for, said they, our fathers, yes, and we ourselves, have lain often upon straw pallets, on rough mats only covered with a sheet, under covers made of rough skins, with a good round log under their heads instead of a bolster or pillow. . . . Pillows, they said, were thought fit only for women in childbed.

The third thing they tell of is the change in vessels, as from wooden platters into pewter, and wooden spoons into silver or tin. For so common was all sorts of wooden stuff in old times that a man could hardly

find four pieces of pewter . . . in a good farmer's house. And yet, for all this careful living . . . they were scarce able to live and pay their rents without selling a cow, or a horse, or more.

Where did the money come from for the changes William Harrison saw? The growing number of people in towns and an increase in industry and trade (see pages 60-61) meant there was much more demand for what farmers grew. People needed *food*, and industry needed *raw materials* like wool, skins and flax. Tudor farmers began to grow *cash crops* most suited to their area. **B** is a map of farming regions in the south east of England.

1 Look carefully at the list of goods a Tudor yeoman owned (pages 44-45). Write down which of them his family would have owned fifty years earlier. Use William Harrison's account for clues.

2 If you walked through Islip in 1527, and again in 1587, what would be the main differences you might see in the village?

3 Look at **B**. Account for the differences in farming between the areas on the map.

THE TUDOR TOWN 1

A *It is a wife's job . . . to ride or go to the market, to sell butter, cheese, milk, eggs, chickens, capons, hens, pigs, geese, and all manner of corns. And also to buy all manner of necessary things for the household.*

So continued the description of the Tudor yeoman's wife. What could Thomas and Alice Campion (see pages 44-45) buy, sell or get done in the town? The larger and wealthier the area that the town served the greater the choice of services on offer, see table **B**.

A survey of Coventry in 1522 and tax lists for Northampton and Leicester help us work out the number of people who did different jobs in large Tudor towns, see **C**.

What impact do you think changes in farming

B

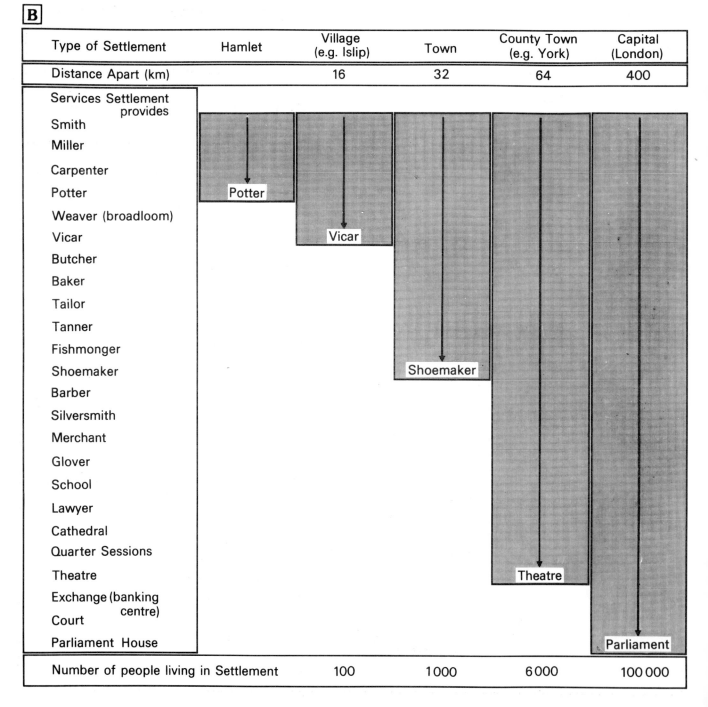

Type of Settlement	Hamlet	Village (e.g. Islip)	Town	County Town (e.g. York)	Capital (London)
Distance Apart (km)		16	32	64	400

Services Settlement provides:
Smith, Miller, Carpenter, Potter, Weaver (broadloom), Vicar, Butcher, Baker, Tailor, Tanner, Fishmonger, Shoemaker, Barber, Silversmith, Merchant, Glover, School, Lawyer, Cathedral, Quarter Sessions, Theatre, Exchange (banking centre), Court, Parliament House

| Number of people living in Settlement | 100 | 1000 | 6000 | 100 000 |

(pages 48-49), the growth in population, the increase in trade and industry (pages 60-61) meant for Tudor towns? **D** gives some clues — it shows a Tudor town in 1610. Towns such as **D** relied on people using rivers, roads and tracks to reach it. Map **B** on pages 58-59 shows the main Tudor towns, roads and waterways.

C

Coventry		Northampton		Leicester	
Cappers	83	Shoemakers	50	Butchers	27
Weavers	41	Bakers	21	Shoemakers	24
Shearmen	38	Tailors	20	Tailors	18
Butchers	36	Weavers	20	Mercers	16
Shoemakers	28	Tanners	15	Weavers	16
Drapers	28	Mercers	15	Bakers	15
Dyers	28	Butchers	14	Tanners	11
Bakers	27	Glovers	13	Glovers	10
Mercers	26	Fullers	12	Smiths	7
Tailors	21	Drapers	9	Millers	7
Tanners	15	Dyers	9	Barbers	7
Smiths	14	Millers	9	Shearmen	7

? ? ? ? ? ? ? ? ? ? ?

1 What size town would provide these services:
   a weaver; tailor; tanner;
   b lawyer; cathedral; quarter sessions;
   c miller; baker;
   d theatre; court?

2 Look at the street names of Shrewsbury on **D**. Write down the different services these streets provided. Say what kind of town you think Shrewsbury was, and what services it might provide for a yeoman and his wife on their visits to it.

3 Use **B** on this page and the information on pages 52-53 of *The Normans* to say how towns changed from 1100 to 1600 AD.

D

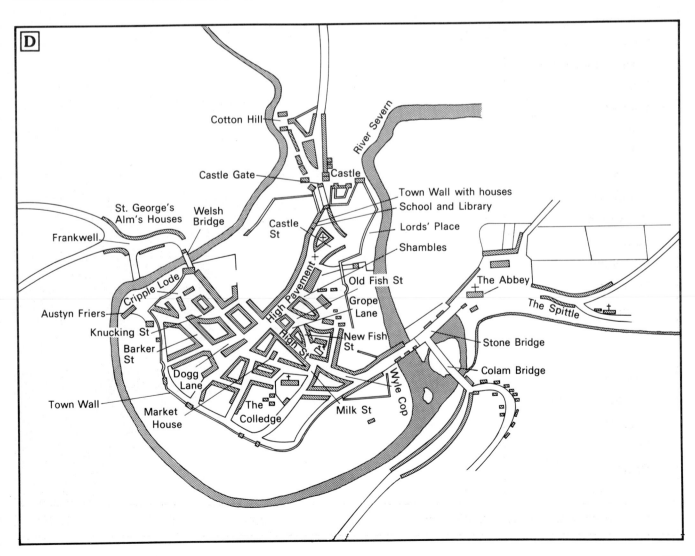

THE TUDOR TOWN 2

If Alice Campion had visited Shrewsbury in 1600, what might she have seen? Imagine that she approached the Castle Gate (see **D**, pages 52-53). What might the new houses outside the walls suggest? When she went through the gate, she would notice other changes from the last hundred years. On her right was the new school house. In 1552, a Shrewsbury man wrote that the town council had asked the king for £20 a year:

A . . . *towards the maintenance of a free school in the said town of Shrewsbury for ever, which was obtained to the great benefit of the youth of that town and the surrounding areas for good learning and godly education. Which schoolhouse is situated near the castle gate. . . .*

B shows a scene in a school like Shrewsbury's.

Although the streets were filthy, Alice noticed that they were paved. The paving was not worn, and seemed to be newly laid. When she reached the High Street, she had a drink from a fountain. The Shrewsbury man wrote in 1572:

C . . . *the conduit water of Shrewsbury was brought in leaden pipes . . . into the upper end of Shoemaker Row, and the great cistern of lead was . . . finished.*

Alice reached the end of High Pavement, passed the market stalls, and saw on her left the new market house. It was in the middle of the town square. Four years earlier the town council had agreed:

D . . . *to take down the old building in the Cornmarket, and sell the timber work thereof to certain of the town's men, and with all speed to . . . build in the place with stone and timber a sumptuous hall, a loft and a large market house for corn beneath.*

E

G

After Alice had bought some cloth in the market square — see an early photograph **E** — she went past the Shambles — the butchers' shops — to the cross at the end of High Pavement. Here she sold her eggs under the brand-new:

F . . . *timber-work for country folk and others to sit and stand dry from rain to sell their poultry, butter, eggs and cheese.*

Before going home Alice decided to visit a friend from her village who had moved to Shrewsbury. She lived at the bottom of Wyle Cop. **G** shows an historic house in Wyle Cop. Notice the first floor window which had only been discovered in 1889. Perhaps King Henry VII slept there on his way to Bosworth field. (See pages 4-5.)

As she passed down the Wyle Cop, Alice noticed the pole to which bulls and bears were chained when dogs were set on them. Then, according to our Shrewsbury writer:

H *Thomas Evans of Oswestry, a gentleman, was shamefully murdered on the Wyle Cop, near the Red Lion, by one Richard Twisse, a trumpeter and servant to one Master Williams. Which Twisse came behind the said Evans while he fought with one Emery, a friend of Twisse, and thrust him through the body with a rapier . . . with*

great speed he passed on horseback through the town and across the ford at Frankwell. . . . Twisse was pursued with hue and cry but could not be overtaken.

1 Use the evidence on these pages and table **B** on pages 52-53 to draw up a list of the things you think Alice would have been able to buy in Shrewsbury in 1587. Shrewsbury was a *county* town — the capital of Shropshire.

2 Write a story as if you were with Alice on her trip to Shrewsbury. You could make it in the form of a letter home to say what Shrewsbury was like. Use these ideas to help you: houses; streets; rubbish; smells; paving; market square; piped water; cloth; merchant's house; butchers' shops; selling eggs and butter; Wyle Cop; hue and cry; blood.

3 On your own map of Shrewsbury, mark the route which Alice took through the town.

4 Look at **B**. How different is the teaching of the pupils from what you experience?

LONDON 1

A is what Thomas Platter, a German tourist, saw from the side of the River Thames opposite the Tower of London in 1599. On the left is the end of London Bridge. Thomas noted:

> **B** *The bridge across the river is of squared stone, very long and with twenty arches. On the top of one tower, almost in the centre of the bridge, were stuck on tall stakes more than thirty skulls of noblemen who had been executed and beheaded for treason and for other reasons. . . . On the same bridge . . . are many tall, handsome merchant dwellings and expensive shops, where all manner of wares are for sale, as in a long street.*

He tells us:

> **C** *. . . it is more usual to cross the water or travel up and down the river by attractive pleasure craft, for a number of tiny streets lead to the Thames from both sides and ends of the town. The boatmen wait here in great crowds, each eager to be the first to catch a passenger. . . .*

Thomas hired a boat for this trip to the Tower of London.

> **D** *We first entered an armoury where were many coats of armour, weapons and pikes. There we were shown King Henry's armour, which was very heavy. . . .*

During his stay, Thomas went to the theatre, to a cock-fight and to bear baiting. **E** is part of a map which shows where they were held. At the bear baiting Thomas tells us:

> **F** *. . . a large bear on a long rope was tied*

to a stake. Then many great English bulldogs were brought in and first shown to the bear which afterwards they baited one after another. The excellence and guts of such bulldogs were shown, for although they were much struck and mauled by the bear, they did not give in, but had to be pulled off by sheer force and their mouths kept open with long sticks with a broad iron-piece fixed to the top. The bear's teeth were not sharp, and could not injure the dogs. . . .

G shows a meal in an inn. Thomas remarked on the:

H . . . great many inns, taverns and beer-gardens scattered about the city, where much amusement may be had in eating, drinking, fiddling and the rest. In the ale-houses, you can buy tobacco — a species of ground wort — and the powder is lit in a small pipe.

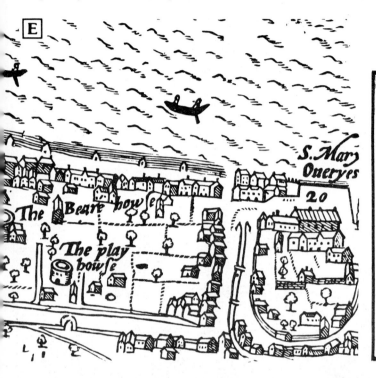

1 What would Thomas Platter have seen at the points marked **a**; **b**; **c**; **d**; **e**; **f**; **g**; and **h** on **A**?

2 Use evidence **E**, **F** and **G** to write a story about an evening's entertainment in London, with a visit to a tavern and the bear pit, *or* draw picture **G** with detailed notes on what is going on in it.

3 How reliable are the sources on this page as historical evidence?

LONDON 2: TRADE AND GROWTH

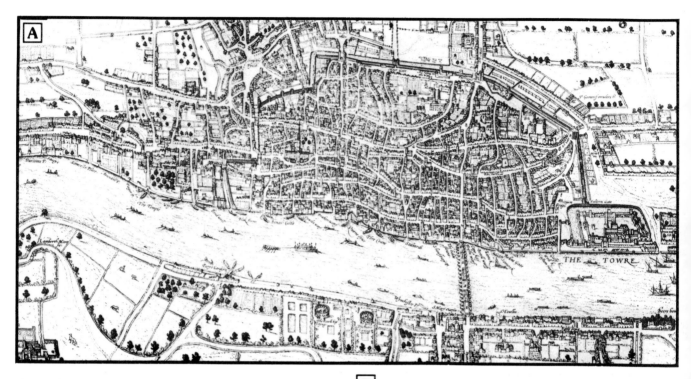

A is a bird's eye view of London in about 1599, **B** a clue of why it was the capital city of England. Thomas Platter provides evidence about London's wealth. Downstream from London Bridge, he said:

> **C** *Ocean craft run in here in great numbers, as it is a safe harbour. I myself saw one large ship after another over the whole city's length, from St Catherine's suburb to the Bridge, some hundred vessels in all.*

He noted the business life of London:

> **D** *Most of the inhabitants are employed (work) in commerce. They buy, sell and trade in all the corners of the globe, for which purpose the water serves them well, since ships from France, the Netherlands, Germany and other countries dock in this city. They bring with them goods that they exchange for others that they load for export.*
>
> *There are also many wealthy merchants, money changers and bankers in this city. Some of them sell expensive goods, while others deal only in money or wholesale goods.*

B **Roads and Rivers used for Travel, 1600**

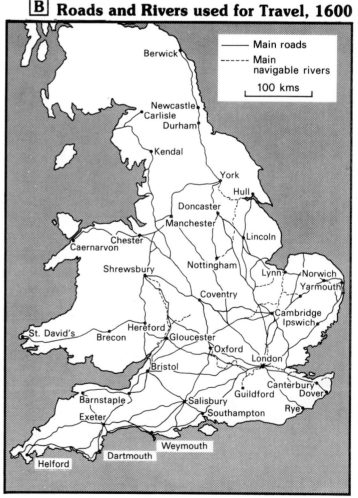

Main roads

Main navigable rivers

100 kms

Berwick
Newcastle
Carlisle
Durham
Kendal
York
Hull
Doncaster
Manchester
Lincoln
Chester
Caernarvon
Shrewsbury
Nottingham
Lynn
Norwich
Yarmouth
Coventry
Cambridge
Ipswich
St. David's
Hereford
Brecon
Gloucester
Oxford
London
Bristol
Canterbury
Guildford
Dover
Barnstaple
Salisbury
Rye
Exeter
Southampton
Weymouth
Helford
Dartmouth

Different parts of the city made and sold special goods.

E *On either side of one very long street called Cheapside live almost only gold-smiths and money-changers.*

Thomas visited the trading and banking heart of the City, the Exchange, **F**:

F

H **Export of Cloth, 1500-05**

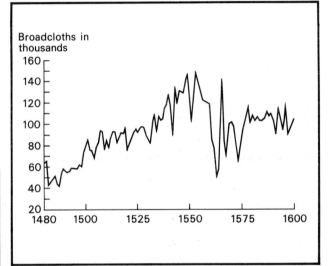

Number of wool broadcloths

20 000
10 000
0

100 kms

Newcastle •

Hull •
Boston •
Lynn
Norwich
Ipswich
London •
Sandwich •
Bristol •
Bridgwater
Southampton •
Chichester
Exeter •
Poole
Plymouth

G *The Exchange is a great square place like the one in Antwerp, a little smaller though, and with only two entrances and a passage running through it, where all kinds of fine goods are on show. Since the city is very large merchants who have to do business agree to meet here.*

Several hundred may gather daily, before lunch at eleven and again after their meal at six o'clock, buying, selling, bearing news and doing business generally.

Cloth stayed as London's most important export. **H** shows its relative importance in 1500, and **J** what happened to it from 1485-1600.

J **Export of Broadcloths, 1485-1600**

Broadcloths in thousands

160
140
120
100
80
60
40
20

1480 1500 1525 1550 1575 1600

? ? ? ? ? ? ? ? ? ?

1 Describe scene **F**, and say what people there are doing.

2 An idea of how important a town is can be gained from counting how many roads and rivers ran to it. Using map **B**, put the following places into order of importance: Barnstaple; Brecon; Bristol; Coventry; Gloucester; Lincoln; London; Shrewsbury; Yarmouth.

3 What does **H** tell us about London's wealth in 1500?

4 Use the evidence on these pages to say how wealthy and important London was in 1600, and how it had changed since 1500.

TUDOR INDUSTRY

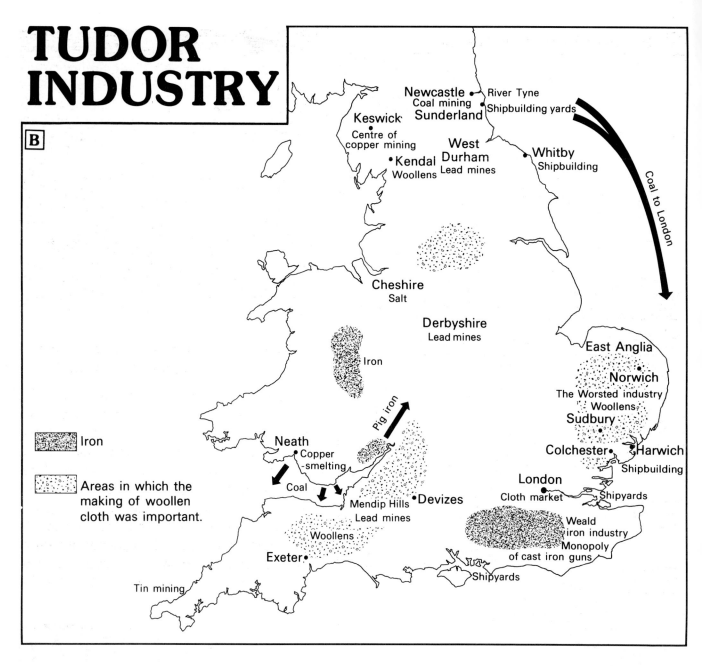

B

Newcastle
Coal mining

River Tyne

Sunderland

Shipbuilding yards

Keswick
Centre of
copper mining

West
Durham
Lead mines

Whitby
Shipbuilding

•Kendal
Woollens

Coal to London

Cheshire
Salt

Derbyshire
Lead mines

East Anglia

Norwich

The Worsted industry
Woollens

Sudbury

Iron

Pig iron

Colchester•

Harwich

Shipbuilding

Neath
•Copper
-smelting

London
Cloth market

Shipyards

Coal

Mendip Hills
Lead mines

•Devizes

Weald
iron industry
Monopoly
of cast iron guns

Iron

Woollens

Areas in which the
making of woollen
cloth was important.

Exeter•

Shipyards

Tin mining

Thomas Campion cursed. It had been a day of disaster. The copper cooking pot had finally burnt through, and was ruined. Alice had singed his two best shirts while drying them over the fire. Where would he get a new copper cooking pot and shirts? He would have to take a day off work and visit the county town to buy them from shopkeepers or stall-holders. They sold goods that they got from Tudor industrialists. Industrialists employed people who usually worked in their own homes (cottage industries) or in small factories.

By 1587 Thomas Campion was able to buy many more industrial goods than his great grandfather in 1500. Why was this? By 1587 there was a growth in *demand* because of increased trade to old markets, particularly Europe, and newly discovered lands –

America and the Indies. At home the growth of towns and changes in farming meant that more industrial products were sold. A typical example was the use of coal. A Tudor writer tells us about the trade in coal by 1587:

A *. . . their greatest trade is now moving from the forge to the kitchen and hall, as appears already in most cities and towns . . . near the coast, where they have but little other fuel.*

B shows Tudor industries in about 1600. To make iron you needed charcoal, ironstone and limestone, and a stream to power the furnace's bellows and the forge's hammers. **C** is a map of iron forges and furnaces in England's most important iron making area – the Weald of Kent. **D** gives an idea of charcoal making. The

C Furnaces in South-east England

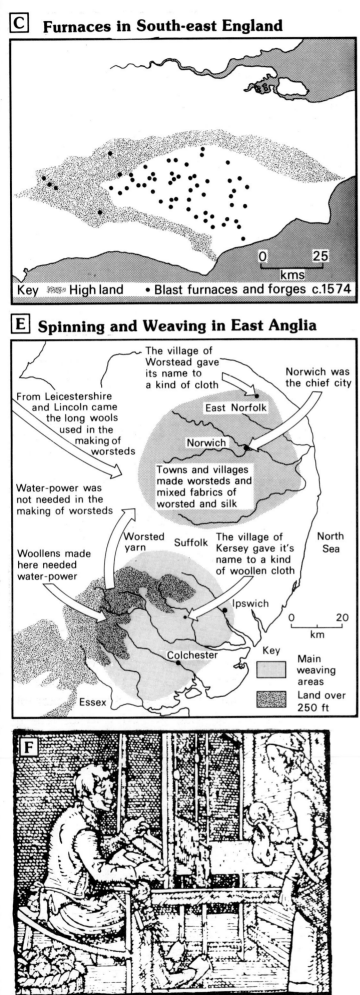

Key ▨ High land • Blast furnaces and forges c.1574

0 — 25 kms

E Spinning and Weaving in East Anglia

The village of Worstead gave its name to a kind of cloth

Norwich was the chief city

East Norfolk

From Leicestershire and Lincoln came the long wools used in the making of worsteds

Norwich

Towns and villages made worsteds and mixed fabrics of worsted and silk

Water-power was not needed in the making of worsteds

Worsted yarn   Suffolk   The village of Kersey gave it's name to a kind of woollen cloth

North Sea

Woollens made here needed water-power

Ipswich

0 — 20 km

Colchester

Key
▨ Main weaving areas
▨ Land over 250 ft

Essex

wood burns very slowly inside the stack when it is covered with straw, green leaves and turf.

The most important Tudor industry was the weaving of woollen cloth for export. **E** shows a major wool cloth making region. Different kinds of cloth were made in different ways. Some woollens needed the water-power of local streams, others could be made without it. Wool was first spun into thread, and then woven in weavers' homes – like **F**. The cloth was sold in rolls to merchants, who then treated it further – either washing, dying or clipping it. The finished cloth was usually sent to London for export to Europe.

??????????????

1 Where, in 1587, would the following goods which Thomas Campion could buy in his local market have been mined or made: raw iron; tin; worsted cloth; copper pot; salt; lead pipe; coal.

2 Use **D** and **F** to describe how charcoal and wool cloth were made.

3 What impact do you think the making of iron had upon the Sussex landscape? A Tudor writer tells us:

> **G** *A forge and furnace yearly use 1000 loads of charcoal, which amounts to 3000 cart-loads of wood, . . .*

4 Use the evidence above to write an account of Tudor industry in 1600.

SEA DOG!

28th August 1595 You represent the captain of one of the ships about to sail with Sir Francis Drake and John Hawkins to visit the colony of Virginia in North America to see if there are any survivors, and to attack the Spanish town of Panama in the Indies for gold and silver. **The object of the game** is to sail to Virginia, and then attack Panama and return to Plymouth. **The winner** is the first ship back to Plymouth. **To play the game** – follow the rules.

Rules

Up to four people can play. A coin or counter represents your ship. To play, take turns in the alphabetical order of your surnames. When it is your turn, place your ship in the Plymouth square. Toss a coin and use the list below to see what has happened to your ship for that turn. The **numbers** refer to the areas on the map.

For each of your following moves move the ship to any area next to the one it is in at present, either horizontally or diagonally. **The winner** is the captain who sails to Virginia, then to Panama and is first back to Plymouth.

Keep a log or diary of your journey. Each turn equals one week. In your log say what has happened to you that week, and how the voyage is going. **A week's delay** means that you miss a move. Each move you make represents a week.

When the ship returns to England, its cargo will be sold, and profit left divided between a group of court gentlemen like Sir Richard Warren, who paid for the ship and its voyage.

---

1   *Heads:* Your ships are ready to sail, and the fleet can leave port.
     Tails: The ships are short of supplies, and cannot leave for a week.

2   *Heads:* A strong following wind means you make good progress.
     Tails: Strong headwinds, and you are blown back to your last square.

3   *Heads:* You have landed in Greenland, and take fresh water on board. You also manage to catch some fresh fish.
     Tails: A tribe of eskimoes attacks. You are delayed for a week.

4   *Heads:* You have entered a shoal of flying fish. These supply you with fresh food which keeps the crew healthy.
     Tails: Typhoid has broken out on board. You anchor for a week, and are delayed.

5   *Heads:* You get fresh supplies in the Cape Verde Islands. The crew is in good spirits.
     Tails: A Spanish fleet has attacked you while at anchor. You are delayed a week repairing the damage.

6   *Heads:* A storm blows your ship on. No damage occurs.
     Tails: You are surrounded by icebergs. Progress is slow, and your journey is delayed for a week.

7   *Heads:* The weather is extremely hot, but a slight wind blows you on.
     Tails: The weather is very hot, and you are becalmed. Water is running out. You are delayed for a week.

8   *Heads:* You hold religious services on board to keep the crew happy.
     Tails: A crew member has died, and you bury him at sea. A week's delay.

9   *Heads:* You reach Virginia to find the colony deserted, and immediately sail on.
     Tails: You reach Virginia and find the colony deserted. Search parties are sent out, which delay your journey by a week.

10   *Heads:* You manage to capture a Spanish treasure galleon.
     Tails: The Spanish treasure galleon fights you off, and you put into local harbour to repair the damage. A week's delay.

11   *Heads:* You find Panama strongly defended. The fleet attacks but is beaten off. You escape in your ship.
     Tails: Drake has failed in the attack on Panama, and has died at sea. Your ship is safe, but you delay a week while making repairs and waiting for the rest of the fleet to join you.